BR[OK]EN

OVERCOMING THE OBSTACLES OF LIFE

BR[OK]EN

OVERCOMING THE OBSTACLES OF LIFE

JASON
MITCHELL

XULON PRESS

Xulon Press
2301 Lucien Way #415
Maitland, FL 32751
407.339.4217
www.xulonpress.com

Paperback ISBN-13: 978-1-66286-492-6
Ebook ISBN-13: 978-1-66286-493-3

br(OK)en: Overcoming The Obstacles of Life

Details in some anecdotes and stories have been changed to protect the identities of the persons involved.

To anyone who has struggled in life, faced challenges, and has been counted out. You are an overcomer and I pray this book helps you through your challenges and situations you may be going through during this day and time of the ever changing world that we live in!

Contents

CHAPTER 1

The Story Begins:

GROWING UP FATHERLESS, I was bound to be another black statistic. However, this story may surprise you as the outcome is very different. See, my dad was black, and my mother was mixed with all kinds of ethnicities. This is why people don't know if I'm Black, Puerto Rican, Mexican, Indian, or just a mix of everything under the sun. I saw my biological father, but I never really knew him. The only memory I have of him is from when I was two years old. It was a dark, late night, and as most two-year-olds often do, I was walking around the living room in my diapers. There was stuff on the small glass table, but I knew not to touch it. It was white powder and beer cans. At this age, I didn't know what it was, but I do know it wasn't anything good for me. That gloomy night, all I remember hearing was yelling and screaming, and it wasn't anything pleasant but a vivid memory that sticks in my mind to this day. My dad and my mom arguing upstairs were very loud, and we were in a small Italian apartment in Italy where they were stationed. I looked upstairs and saw my mom and dad by the edge of the steps. He was hitting her and grabbed her by the arm, shaking her harshly. My dad was high and drunk, as he often was every night. Every night was the same old scene of yelling, fighting, and arguing.

On this night, he grabbed my mom by her neck, and I could see the scared look on her face, with tears falling from her eyes. With his hands wrapped around her neck, he threw her down the narrow stairs. I remember seeing her tumbling down the steps, flipping step by step until she reached the bottom. She was hurt, holding her head and arm. I didn't know what to do, but I knew my mom was hurt, so I went over and tried to comfort her. As a two-year-old, there isn't much you can do or provide, but I knew I could make my mom smile, as I always did. This time it didn't seem to work. My dad was always abusive due to his drug and alcohol problems. Every night he would come home yelling, screaming, cursing, and fighting. This isn't the type of memory a kid should have of his dad, but it's the only memory I have.

Both of my parents were in the military, and drugs in the military are a huge violation that can get you kicked out. I don't know. Maybe it was different in the 70s because everyone used to have parties, and things were not the same as they are today. Born in 1976, I can only imagine the kinds of parties that my parents went to and how I was conceived. I'm sure it wasn't planned, and I can almost guarantee it was a wild night out on the town with a lot of alcohol and drugs. Now that I came into the world, all that would suddenly change and disrupt everything my mom and dad would do. I was born as Jason Mitchell in Colorado Springs, Colorado, at Fort Carson on November 13, 1976. I have no memories of this place as I was only a baby. My earliest memory comes from my previous mentions of Italy, where my parents were stationed. They were both in the Army, and from some of the pictures I've seen, they sure loved to party. I can recall, as a little two-year-old, light-skinned, fluffy afro-headed boy, walking around with my shirt off and diapers on, smiling at all the people. I would go around to all the soda cans people put on the table at my parents' small apartment during house parties and drink the remainder of what was left. I would stand by the people and wait for them to get done so I could finish up the soda they had if they didn't drink it all. Yeah, I know. Pretty nasty, huh? It got even nastier when I drank one of the sodas and got a mouthful of cigarette ash. People would always smoke, including my mother, and that's the last time I remember taking any kind of drink from their cans. Eventually, I got braver. When everyone was asleep, I would find my way to the refrigerator. Somehow, I would open the refrigerator. The red bottle seemed to appeal the most to me. I worked until I got the top off and proceeded to drink as much of this red liquid as possible. Sitting on the cold, hard floor, I would then begin to say, "hot, hot, hot!" I picture my mother running into the kitchen, asking what I was doing. I ended up drinking almost a whole bottle of hot sauce as a 2-year-old. Maybe that's the reason I love spicy food so much now.

These memories and moments would not last forever, as the separation was about to occur. Remember the incident I mentioned about my mother being thrown down the steps? Well, later that night, I can recall my mother picking me up and my dad tugging at her trying to pry me out of her hands. Eventually, when everything calmed down, both of my parents asked me who I wanted to live with. After carefully considering everything I remember seeing and how my dad was always yelling, I chose my mom. My dad was furious and stormed out of the house. My mother started scrambling furiously and putting as many clothes in a small suitcase as she could fit. I remember her telling me we had to hurry up and get out of there. I'm not sure where my dad went; it was probably the bar, but we moved rather quickly to leave before he made his way back. There's no telling what would have happened if we were still there when he returned. My mother and I left the apartment and ended up back in the States. The next thing I knew, we were on a Greyhound bus headed to Grand Rapids, Michigan, where my mom and her family were from. She hasn't been home since I was born. I can recall her being labeled the Black Sheep of her family and an outcast because she married a black man and had a mixed baby. We weren't welcomed when we arrived in her hometown, and there was a lot of cursing and yelling going on from her mother. I'm not sure what happened or what drove my mother to join the military and leave home. I'm almost positive there were some kind of feelings between her and her family as well, because there wasn't a wedding and her mother didn't approve of the man she married. She had a lot of brothers who seemed like they liked me and would always play with me. There was a specific incident when we were at my mom's brother's house. He had a big clear see-through ball you could climb into and roll around in. He put me in this ball and wouldn't let me out, and it seemed like I was in this ball forever. Ever since this incident, I have been claustrophobic and have never liked being in tight spaces. My mom didn't agree with her mother on many things at this time, and since her family did not welcome us, we would leave. We would go to the bus station again with our small bags. It seemed like we were always at the greyhound station catching buses to different cities. We were unsure where to go next; we would just get on the bus and head to a different city.

My mom would do what she needed to do to take care of me the best she could. She would always protect me, comfort me, and ensure I had something to eat. She loved RC sodas and onion rings. We didn't have very much money at all, and most of the greyhound bus stations had pimps, prostitutes, druggies, and a lot of homeless people walking to and from the lobby. At the greyhound station, I remember two middle-aged, grimy-looking men approaching my mom. They would stare and point, and I'm sure they weren't approaching her to give her flowers and ask her out on a nice date. These guys were pimps looking for the next victim they could send out on the streets. As a single woman with a child in these locations, you were most likely low on money and would do what you needed to do to make ends meet. I remember my mom talking to these guys. She wasn't gone very long and always tried to keep us safe. We would spend countless nights at these greyhounds and even Amtrak stations with a single thin green military itchy blanket, sleeping on the cold hard floor or hard benches because we had nowhere else to go. We were often on the run because my biological dad would come looking for my mom. He always threatened that he would kill her if he found her. There were times when he showed up out of nowhere and would yell at my mom, trying to get her to come back to him. I have no clue how he found us, but I remember one instance of him grabbing my mom around her neck and threatening her life. We managed to get away from him many times, and I think he finally got tired of trying to find us and gave up trying to get my mom back. One of the reasons could have been because of my mom's brothers. It seemed like when we ended up back in Michigan again, this was the last time I saw or heard anything about my dad. I can almost guarantee my mom's brothers threatened my dad's life if he didn't stay away from my mom. My mom's brothers were tough guys and always willing to fight. They loved their baby sister, but the feud between my mom and grandma caused division between everyone. Back in Michigan, we stayed at my grandma's house a few times. Michigan seemed like it always had snow. I loved football and would always play outside and build snowmen and piles of snow. I would pretend to be a running back needing to make it to the end zone. I would grab my football and jump over the snow into the end zone. It was cold, but I didn't care because I was going to be the next Walter Payton when I grew up. After I played football by myself, I would get thirsty. My mom had spare change that she would give me to get RC soda and funyuns from 7-11. 7-11 was about a block away, and I would walk there to get some candy, funyuns, and RC soda for my mom. I am not sure why I would be walking there by myself at the age of 5 or 6, but I do remember it. One of the main reasons I can remember is because one particular day, I was walking there, and in the parking lot was a long, gray car. I'm not sure of the make or model, but an average-built white guy about 6 feet tall got out of the car as I got close to the sidewalk. He approached me, asking me questions about my name and where I lived. He asked me if I wanted to go with him because he had a lot of candy and toys that I could play with. I liked candy and especially toys, as I didn't have any for myself. The only toys I had were my cousin's Star Wars toys that I would get to play with when I was at my grandma's house. As I started walking with him back to his car, my uncle pulled up, jumped out of the car, and started confronting the guy. Police cars pulled into the 7-11 shortly after, and the man was put in handcuffs in the back of a police car. I didn't realize how close I was to being kidnapped on this day. There's no telling what would have happened to me if my uncle was not there at that moment. When my mom found out about what happened, she was furious. Once again, we packed and headed back on the road.

CHAPTER 2
Moving Forward

AS WE MADE it to another city, Harrisburg, Pennsylvania, my mom got a small apartment and worked as a waitress at two fast food places. She would have to work long shifts, and I remember her being so tired that all she could do was sleep when she got home from work. The apartment wasn't anything great, but rather something for us to live in until she could get back on her feet. There were cockroaches that would come from under the cabinets and behind the cracks in the walls. I can even remember opening a cereal box and seeing them move between the cornflakes. It was better than being in a harsh environment, and this time I knew we would at least be safe. Often, when my mom would have to go to work, she would have to leave me in the apartment by myself. There was no furniture, no TV, barely or sometimes not even any food in the refrigerator. She would tell me to stay in the apartment, don't leave, and don't answer the door for anybody. I listened. To keep my mind from wandering, I would play with the few small toys I had to keep me occupied until she returned. At that time, I liked football cards and collected as many as possible. I would occupy myself by pretending to play football games with the cards, lining them up into teams and players, and making my own football field on the cold, hard living room floor. I would run plays and let my imagination take me as far away as possible. It wasn't my mom's fault that she had to leave me there. She was barely making minimum wage and couldn't afford to have somebody watch me. She was barely making ends meet. I would get happy and excited to see her come home from work only to fall asleep because she was exhausted. It was OK, though. She always brought me french fries and burgers from the fast food places she worked at. My favorite food was from Jack In The Box because she would bring me the toys that went in the meals. At the time, they had the best toys. Mom nicknamed me "Little Fry" because I always ate french fries; it was my favorite food. Every time I wanted something to eat, it was always french fries. Although mom was always tired, it was fine because she was working as hard as she could to support us. Maybe when she woke up, we could spend time together. Unfortunately, when she woke up, it was the same routine again. There were a couple of times we went out, and I can remember being on a porch at someone's house that my mom was visiting in Harrisburg. As I was playing, I heard some yelling about six houses down and across the street. As I watched what was happening, I saw two men wearing ski masks. One of the men pulled out a gun, pointed it at the guy on the porch, and shot him. I saw the man look at me and started coming my way. I didn't know what to do, so I laid down like I was dead, and after a few minutes, I got up. I didn't see any signs of these men. Shortly after, the house was taped off with yellow police tape, and a lot of police cars were on the road. Shortly after this incident happened, my mom returned and started packing our clothes again. She told me we were leaving and everything was going to be alright.

Although she quit working at the fast food places, Mom finally made enough money for us to catch an Amtrak to Dallas. She wanted to avoid the Greyhound as much as possible due to all the illegal activity and dangerous situations at those stations. The Amtrak was the next level up from the Greyhound and was a little safer. I will never forget the smell of Amtrak. The smell of old seats and mothballs filled the trains. I used to hate that smell. To me, the Greyhound buses had a better smell than the Amtrak's did. The good thing about Amtrak was that it didn't stop as frequently as the Greyhound buses. This made the trip a little more pleasant, not to mention I could walk back and forth on the train without anyone bothering me. On our trip, I recall my mom saying she wasn't feeling good and sweat filled her face as if she had run a marathon. She told me to see if they had some ice and to try to find someone to help her. I went through the train and found some ice but didn't know who could help her. I didn't see any doctors or nurses on the train. I came back, and she passed out a few minutes later. Some people sitting next to us also saw her pass out and called for help. The train ended up making a stop in a small town. We didn't know anyone there, and I didn't know what was going to happen next. It was just my mom and me. We didn't have any family or anyone else that could help us. I was trying to hold her and take care of her as much as possible until the ambulance arrived. Once they arrived, they took my mom to the hospital. However, I couldn't go in the ambulance with her. The Amtrak workers tried to see if someone there could watch after me until we could find out what was going on with my mom because they had to get back on their schedule. An older couple took me in and brought me to their house until everything was settled. This couple didn't say much to me, but they offered me a small meal and kept asking when someone would come to get me. They would ask where our family was, and the only thing I could tell them was, "In Michigan." Of course, I didn't know any family members' phone numbers, but eventually, they got a call that my mom was OK and that they could bring me to the hospital to see her. My mom asked me how I was doing and if I was OK. I told her I was fine. She said she was proud of me for taking care of her. I was just a little kid, so I did my best. I knew I couldn't cry and had to be brave for my mom when she was going through the situation on the train. I still don't know what happened to this day, but eventually, everything worked out, and we were back on another train headed to Dallas.

Once we arrived in Dallas, my mom met a lady that picked us up from the train station. I didn't know who this lady was. I had never seen her before, but maybe my mom knew her. Maybe it was one of her old Army friends. We stayed with this lady while my mom tried to get back on her feet. She lived in an apartment and seemed to love the church for some reason. She was always at the church throughout the week and, of course, on Sunday. I loved staying with this lady because she always had the coolest toys a boy could ask for. She even brought me a box full of all the dopest toys. I can remember it was close to Christmas time, and maybe this was one of the reasons she had all of these toys. It didn't matter because it seemed like everything was getting better. One of my favorite toys that she gave me was He-Man! This was one of the hottest toys on the market at the time, and everyone wanted one of them. She also got me a little drum set that I loved. Although I loved the drum set, I took that He-Man with me everywhere I went. Since this lady always went to church, she offered an invitation for my mom to attend as well. This was the first time I remember going to a church. The church was called the Christian House of Prayer and led by Daddy McCullough. I don't know how I remember this man's name to this day, but I remember he would always smile and even speak with me sometimes. Daddy McCullough would also let me play in the church band at the beginning of service. We would line up on the side of the aisles with the drummers and various instruments. They would let me line up with them with my little snare toy drum. As the committee walked through the aisle, we played our instruments and songs as the people clapped and cheered. As a kid, this was an awesome feeling because it seemed like a big family and everyone was so happy. I would often glance over the pews and see my mom clapping and singing. She would look at me, smile, and continue praising. I'm not sure what kind of church this was, but people would always go to the front, where there were wood chips and buckets right before the main stage. The people would kneel, and all of them were crying and throwing up these wood chips. They acted as if this was normal. I had never seen anything like this, so I was curious and observant. I was clueless about what was happening, and it was different than anything I had seen before in my short life.

One Sunday at this church, my mom decided we would get baptized. I can remember her holding me in her arms and both of us being baptized at the same time in a large swimming pool. It seemed like my mom was very happy, and these people from the church were helping her start a new life. This was my first encounter with a church. It didn't last long. My mom would always keep a Bible with her everywhere we went. Whenever I had nightmares or bad dreams, she would put it under my pillow and rub some oil over my head. Whenever I didn't feel good, she would do the same thing, and eventually, I would feel better. I didn't understand what putting a Bible under my pillow was supposed to do then, but my mom's faith in Jesus kept us safe and healthy during these years. Things were moving forward, and it was beginning to seem like life was getting better. My mom seemed happy; we weren't sleeping in Greyhound bus stations or shelters anymore, and we would eat some real food now and then.

Maybe I spoke too soon. Once again, I found myself getting woken up in the middle of the night. My mom was packing again and dragged me out of bed. She told me to get dressed quickly because we had to leave. I don't know what happened, but I don't think she and the lady were friends anymore. We ended up heading down to the all-too-familiar Greyhound bus station. My mom purchased another ticket, but we didn't stay there this time as we did at the other stations. We went around the corner and checked into a female Salvation Army sleeping center. We stayed there that night, and my mom told me to make sure I stayed close to her at all times. We snuggled up with our one blanket and went to sleep. The next morning, we woke up, got dressed, and walked around the corner to the Greyhound bus station. I didn't have much, and my mom had one bag. All I remember having was a change of clothes and my favorite He-Man toy. It seemed like having this toy kept my mind off the reality of sadness and depression happening all around me. As long as I had this toy and my mom, nothing could take my joy. Once it was time to start loading the bus, my mom and I walked up the stairs and proceeded down the aisle. We found a seat about halfway down the bus and sat down. Shortly after we sat down, my mom asked me if I needed to use the bathroom. We both got up and walked down the aisle to the back of the bus, where the bathrooms were located.

I left my He-Man and sweatshirt on the seat, not thinking anything could happen to them. About 5 to 6 people were close to our seats, and they seemed to be a little rowdy. They were all together and ranged in age from about 18 to 24 years old. It was a mix of males and females. I can remember them making a lot of noise, laughing and joking. As we were walking back to our seats, we passed this group of young people, and I saw them laughing and whispering. Once we returned to our seats, I noticed my He-Man was missing. I looked everywhere, including under the seat and on the floor. There was no He-Man in sight. The only thing I had to hold onto to keep my mind off the pain and anger I was experiencing was no longer there. These people took my only toy. The worst part is that they didn't have any remorse. My mom was extremely mad and was trying to find out who had taken it, but she didn't have any luck. It was gone, and we were headed to our next destination.

CHAPTER 3
The Odd Life

I'VE TRAVELED TO so many places on this bus that I don't even recall where we ended up next. My mom met a guy named Joe Watson at a local bar in the city where we stopped. They seemed to get along well, and the next thing I knew, we were always together with this guy. I remember seeing him drinking a lot of beer and smoking these funny-looking cigarettes. This guy was really big and had an afro similar to what I remember from my dad. I was used to being the only guy in my mom's life, and now we've got this guy hanging around all the time. One day, my mom and I wound up leaving with this guy, and there was no telling where we would end up next. I was still traveling and switching schools as often as some people changed their underwear. It seemed like normal life to me. I would attend a school, and about a couple of months later, we would pack up and leave for the next city. I was already used to moving my whole life, and now we were doing it again with this stranger my mom barely knew.

Depending on what state I was in, the kids talked and dressed differently. Of course, I was the new kid on the block every time I switched schools, so I would have to prove myself by fighting or being the class clown just to try to fit in. This would be my way of trying to make new friends and showing people that I was cool too. Even in 2nd grade in Michigan, I remember forming a 25-kid gang and leading a huge brawl during recess. I was the cool kid at that school because I was running things even in 2nd grade. How can you even form a gang in 2nd grade? I don't know, but I did it. At this same school, I was even able to play "house" for the first time. Yes, in 2nd grade, I was in the playhouse feeling on girls' butts and kissing them on the lips because I was the daddy and they were the mommy. You couldn't tell my friends and me anything, which is why we ran away and were gone for a full day. Eventually, the police and my family found us by the beach in Michigan, but we were cool because we were brave enough to run away. Relocating to me meant nothing anymore, and as I began to get older, it was the norm. I would be at a school for a couple of months and then off to the next state and school. I did not have cool clothes or shoes, so I would try to fit in with the latest music video fashions and trends, which would sometimes get me picked on by other students. Faded jeans with holes and dirty t-shirts didn't help me make many friends. I would quickly get angry and be ready to fight anyone trying to pick on me, which seemed to help me in some instances. The kids would see that I wasn't scared to fight, and finally, I would earn their respect.

We moved all over the country. I went to schools in Little Rock, Houston (Pasadena), North Myrtle Beach, Fort Lauderdale, Tucson, Holland, Grand Rapids, and other smaller towns across the states where we decided to stay. Altogether, I attended about 14–15 different schools growing up. There were times I can remember, like it was yesterday, when we would sleep in a tent at the KOA campgrounds. Other times, I remember sleeping in the back of a U-Haul truck across the street from my school in Houston. I would wake up, put my clothes on, and walk across the street to the school. Two major incidents happened in 1989 that I can remember while attending school. The first was the Phillips Disaster, where the Phillips 66 plant blew up. My school was miles away, but I can remember the roof shaking and the white powder from the ceiling falling on us because the explosion was so powerful. We didn't know what was happening. All the teachers told the students to get down under the desks. We thought it was funny and were glad we were getting out of class. We had no idea that so many people lost their lives due to the chemical explosion on this day. The other incident was Hurricane Hugo, which was one of the most powerful hurricanes in history to hit the United States. We would always follow or end up in these disastrous places because when Joe wasn't dealing drugs, he was into construction. This is how he made his money and supported us. In North Myrtle Beach, after Hurricane Hugo hit, we lived in a motel that had two beds in the room and a small TV. The motel was only a block from the beach. It wasn't anything fancy at all, but I liked this place. This was one of my favorite places because I was into wrestling, football, and video games, and I eventually learned how to surf from my best friend, Willie Vachon. I think I was the only brown-skinned kid in 1989 that tried surfing. At least I was in this area. I got good at surfing, and this helped keep my mind off of everything that was going on within our small family. It was like an escape from the real world to me. I would hang out at the beach every day after school and all day during the summer. Finally, we moved into an actual house about four blocks from the beach, and I had my own room. I never had an actual room, and I was always used to sharing everything with my mom. When my mom and Joe were gone to work, I would practice dance routines and rap to the latest videos on TV, such as Digital Underground's "Humpty Dance." I would always practice rapping and started to get more into it when I wasn't watching wrestling.

Wrestling was my life. I knew every wrestler from the NWA, AWA, and WWF. One day, I went down to the beach and saw two guys and a lady lying on the beach. One of the guys got up and walked towards the beach, and when he turned around, I was in awe! It was one of my favorite wrestlers to watch from the NWA. It was "Rugged" Ronnie Garvin! I ran to the pier right next to where they were located. I went inside to get a pen and paper so I could get his autograph. That was the first time I had ever seen anyone famous. Once I came back down, I started walking towards his towel and wife. He was coming back out of the water, and when he walked up, I asked him if I could have his autograph. It turned into a huge disappointment when he told me to get lost. A grown, iconic wrestler telling me, a 12-year-old kid that only wanted an autograph, to get lost? This only crushed me even more. I remembered walking away with my head down and torn. Every time I watched wrestling, I always hoped Ronnie Garvin would get crushed by every opponent. I hated him now.

I remember going down to the pier at the beach and playing Ikari Warriors until the store closed. I would have a jar full of quarters because my mom worked as a waitress and always gave me her change. I stayed in the water and practiced surfing all day when I wasn't playing video games at the pier's arcade. I would surf so much and be in the water so long that my hair turned light brown or orange. I had a great time, but when school started, I was ashamed for people to know that I stayed in a motel. Although I was ashamed every time the school bus would drop me off in front of the old, crusty motel, this was an amazing place for me as a kid. I even picked the first time Mike Tyson would lose, which was to Buster Douglas in 1990. Mike Tyson was an icon during this timeframe. It was every kid's dream to live a block from the beach. This is also where I met my best friend, Willie Vachon. He would let me stay the night at his house often, and we would pretend to be the latest superstar wrestlers at the time. I would always pick Hawk or Animal from the Road Warriors. We would wrestle so much that one day I had Willie in the pile driver position, and his mom screamed to put him down. I listened and let go, only for Willie to hit his head on the pavement and get a seizure. That would be the last of our wrestling days and the last time I would get to see Willie for a few weeks. His mom was furious. Since I didn't have friends to hang out with, I landed my first job cleaning tables in a restaurant where my mom worked. This money helped support my arcade habit. This was when I started to get even more into Hip Hop, which would begin to start a shift in my life. I would listen to all of the latest music, watch all of the videos and practice all of the latest dances.

At this point, we packed up and moved again. This time it was to another great place, Fort Lauderdale, Florida. Everyone always talked greatly about this place; after all, it was always sunny. I was excited until my first day of school. This place seemed more like a penitentiary than a school. The school was fenced in, and once inside the school, the bathrooms were in the classrooms. This sucked because now you couldn't leave the classroom. There was never anyone in the hallways, and if you were caught in the hallways without a pass, you would get in big trouble. We had a big black lady for a teacher who looked like an NFL linebacker. She was very firm and strict, and she never smiled. If we didn't do our homework, she would take the kids to the bathroom and spank them with a wooden paddle. I thought to myself, "My parents must be crazy for putting me in this school." The best part of the day was when we left school. I would walk home, which was about a half mile. It was a rough neighborhood, and drug dealers flocked the streets. I never had anyone bother me, but from how our school was set up, I could tell we weren't in Disneyland. Even next door to our house, we had a crazy lady banging on our door, yelling, "Let the kids out!" My mom went out the sliding back door in the backyard, and I saw her slap the taste out of the lady's mouth. We didn't see this lady again. Although we lived in another drug-infested neighborhood, it was alright with me because at least they had wrestling here. This was one of the hottest places for the wrestling circuit. All of the up-and-coming wrestlers came from this area. I got to see some of the wrestling legends for the first time, like Lex Luger and Jimmy "Superfly" Snuka. Besides the pomegranates and grapefruits, this was the best thing happening in this city. It wouldn't last, though, as we hit the road again and headed to Tucson, Arizona. This is where Joe's brother and dad lived. He received a call that his dad was really sick and preparing to pass away. We loaded up in the U-Haul truck and headed out to Arizona. Once we arrived, we moved into a trailer park in another rough area of Southside Tucson. It was an extremely rough area, especially the trailer park we stayed in. Drugs and gangs infested this area both day and night. Every day was a battle to walk home from the bus safely. This was my first real encounter with a bully that thought he owned the whole park. He would always try to throw spitballs at a few of us and threaten to shoot us all of the time. Being used to this type of environment didn't scare me, but I was tired of being bullied and worrying if I would make it home every day. Once, I stood up to this guy after we got off the bus. He started to back down from me, but continued bullying other kids. I was never a big kid, but I was skinny and could come off as a little crazy because I didn't have a care in the world. Plus, I watched wrestling and knew all of the moves. It probably wouldn't have helped me much, but in my mind at the time, I thought it would.

This is also where I learned to hustle even more, but thank God it wasn't drugs. I would get bags of candy from the corner store with a lot of Mexican candy, Now & Laters, Sugar Daddy's, Fireballs, and whatever else was popular at the time and sell them in class. We would make our trades and sell the most products during recess while we played Tether Ball towards the back of the playground. I made some good money for a kid and ended up having to fight the other entrepreneurs at school because of it. Everybody wanted to be the best and only school candy dealer. This was one of the first real fights I had. During recess, we all gathered in the back towards the fence where all the fights went down. There was hardly any talking, and we started pounding each other. I guess I hit him with a good punch because he put his hand up and told me to stop. I still remember seeing all the other kids laughing and pointing at him because he had just gotten beaten by the new kid. We got caught by the teachers, and they took us to the principal's office. I was happy because I had won the fight. I also remember the kid apologizing to me while we were sitting outside the principal's office in the hallway. He was soft while we were sitting in the hallway waiting to see the principal, but once he was around his friends, he lied and said he didn't apologize. He didn't want to seem like a punk around his boys. It was alright, though, because he never messed with me again.

It seemed like trouble was all around this place. Kids would get pulled out of class, and days later, we would find out that they had been sent to the Juvenile Detention Center for criminal activity that they were involved in. I specifically remember seeing about four kids getting pulled out of class and not returning. This was also when I was pulled out of class by some gentleman claiming to be the FBI. They were dressed in suits, Hispanic, clean-shaven, and seemed very serious. They proceeded to ask me questions about where my family was moving next. As a kid, you don't know what's going on. You just go with the flow and do what you're told. I told them I didn't know and that we move every other month or so. These men came back twice and asked me various questions about my parents. This was also the first time I engaged in my first serious illegal activity. One of my so-called friends asked me if I wanted to go to this specific trailer with them. He said the lady kept a lot of money and was never there. He said we could get some money for the candy we sell at school and for anything else we want, like video games. I thought about it and thought it would be a good idea. One day, when the lady wasn't there, we broke into her home and took all her coins in the big plastic water jug she kept. It was almost filled to the top, and she wouldn't even notice it was gone. We thought we got away with a clean robbery. One day, she came home and noticed the money was missing. She told us that she knew it was us. She called the police and snitched on us, but couldn't prove it, so we got away with it.

Reflecting on these times, I can see how kids left in these environments can conform to crime and illegal activities around them. It was a blessing that I could get out of these environments. Going to some places with Joe and my mom, we could have easily ended up getting shot or killed. Southside Tucson was known for illegal activities, drugs, and gangs. Nothing good ever came out of that location. We were blessed to get through there alive and not end up in jail or prison for something that could have easily happened within a split second.

CHAPTER 4
Living Foul

AFTER A COUPLE more moves, we ended up back in Arizona due to Joe's dad passing away. This time, Joe wanted to settle down and said we would be here for a while. It didn't matter to me because I was already used to moving, and it became part of the normal routine that I was used to. Once we settled down and I started school, I immediately connected with this white, slender, tall, cool kid. We would talk about sports and girls all the time. His name was Max Schug, and I could see myself hanging out with this dude. One of the first things we did together was sneak into the girls' locker room. I told Max to keep an eye out. I was going to go in there and look at the naked girls in the locker room. He thought I was crazy, but Max was down for whatever. He stood guard on the wall outside the locker room while I quickly opened the door and went inside. There were girls in there, and they didn't even seem to mind. I saw a few get shocked and quickly wrap a towel around themselves, but they thought it was funny for the most part. I was hanging out in the locker room, telling them jokes and laughing with them. It seemed pretty cool. I could get used to it. Max was alright with me, and now we were inseparable. I came out, and he asked me what had taken so long. I told him what had happened. He couldn't do anything but smile with a devilish grin and give me a dap. He said he wanted to try it next time.

This was my 8th-grade year, and although I had never played sports for an actual team, I loved sports. I could play well, but this was also the time puberty took effect, and my feet were outgrowing my body. I was very clumsy and would trip over my own feet. I don't know how, but I still managed to be one of the coolest black kids in my school. Probably because there weren't many of us, to begin with. This school was mostly made up of Hispanic and Caucasian kids. Most of the kids were cool toward me, and I seemed to get along with everyone. It was a smaller-sized school, and everyone seemed to know each other. This was also when I started getting into hardcore rap music and wrote my first rap to N.W.A.'s "Straight Outta Compton" instrumental. This was when N.W.A., Ice Cube, and Ice-T were very popular, and the new gangster rap music movement was taking over. Everyone was wearing Raiders starter jackets and hats, and gangs were becoming more relevant and noticed. I was serious about my music and loved the message of rebellion that N.W.A. brought into their music. After a few kids heard my song and loved it, there was no turning back. I got myself a red binder specifically for all of my raps. Every rap I wrote was kept in this binder. I had more rap songs than I had schoolwork. This binder was packed and thick compared to my other classwork.

I wasn't a terrible student, but during class, all I did was write my raps and practice my new musical talent at school. I would sit in the back of the classroom, and I would be ready to spit my lyrics during any break we got. There were three girls that I sat next to, and I would always ask them for advice on my songs. Their names were Kristy, Ginger, and Crystal. Kristy would always love the songs I wrote. Crystal would try to pay attention in class, but she didn't want to seem rude and would give me feedback. Ginger, on the other hand, would listen if we had time, but she was very serious about her schoolwork. I wasn't too serious about my schoolwork; however, I excelled in P.E., Spelling, and English classes. I even remember winning the 8th-grade school Spelling Bee. How could an underprivileged kid that didn't pay attention in class but was passionate about writing songs and playing sports win the Spelling Bee? That was odd, but spelling, grammar, and sports always came naturally to me.

Even though I was good in these subjects, Ms. Simms, my English teacher, took my rap binder from me for the entire year. She claimed all I did was write raps and didn't pay attention in class, which was probably true, but taking my binder for the whole year was kind of extreme. Even some of the other students were furious at Ms. Simms for going to that extreme and reported her to the principal. Nothing happened, and my binder was now gone. She told me that I wouldn't make it in life writing rap songs and that I would end up being a failure. This was the all-too-familiar slogan for a lot of black kids, especially during this time and at a school where there weren't too many people with the same skin color as me. At least I can say that I still passed her class! That's something that she couldn't take away from me. I always welcomed challenges, and failure has never been in my vocabulary, especially after everything I went through up to this point in my life. This didn't do anything but make me want to succeed even more and prove to her and every other teacher that they couldn't stop me no matter what they tried to do to me or take from me. To get them back, I joined the school's Talent Show and performed Bobby Brown's "My Prerogative." Although I didn't win, the students loved it, and the teachers got my message. Of course, the teachers were the ones that voted for the winner. I still believe the outcome would have been very different if the students had voted. Although I didn't have my rap binder anymore, I still wrote my songs. I began to get more interested in playing sports. I thought I was pretty good, but, in reality, compared to the other kids, I sucked at all of them, which were football and wrestling at the time.

The main thing was that I wanted to get away from my home life, which was nothing but the smell of weed, people in and out of our house all of the time, drug deals, and working like a slave. See, this was now the early 90s, and most people lived in a normal home with running water, electricity, plumbing, heat, air conditioning, and walls in the house, with a bedroom door and carpet or at least tiles on their floor. This was not the case for my family and me. Joe had some crazy idea of wanting to have a little land and build a house while we lived in it. This guy even had the crazy idea of using billboard signs for the wood! During the summertime in Arizona, it wasn't unusual for the temperature to rise to 110 degrees of pure blazing heat. My mom was pregnant with my little brother, so Joe and I would go to the store to get cement bags, 2x4s, and medium-sized rocks for the rock wall he wanted to build. We would load the truck up with as many supplies as possible, drive back and begin to offload everything. This was also the time that my little brother was finally born. His name is Mason Watson.

He was a big baby, chunky with chubby cheeks. He loved to eat as well. During the summer, while all of the other kids were enjoying their summers and playing or hanging out with friends, I would be working in the hot summer's blazing heat or watching Mason when my mom and Joe went out. We would mix cement with a shovel in a wheelbarrow, push it with a flat tire about 15 yards, and pour it down, creating the cement floor for our house. We would work tirelessly throughout the day, hammering and nailing the 2x4s, making the soon-to-be walls. We would mix more cement to build the rock wall, which looked extremely terrible and old-fashioned in my opinion. When it was time to eat, we would either cook on a grill or start the generator to have electricity for our stove. If we had to use the bathroom, we would fill up a huge pot and pour it into the toilet once we were done so that it could flush properly. At nightfall, I remember having to fill up the generator with fuel so we could have electricity and watch TV. When the gas ran out, I would ride my bike to the corner store and fill up the gas can if we had money to get gas. Was this a normal life for a kid and their family, especially in the 90s?

Sometimes my best friend Max would call during the summer and invite me to sleep over at his house. When I went to his house, it was much different than mine. They had a regular bathroom with a shower and running water, so the toilet would flush. They had doors to all of their rooms; walls in their home instead of blankets hanging up; electricity without having to use a generator; a regular stove for cooking that actually worked; and they even had carpet! I loved staying at their house, and when I wasn't there, I would walk or run to their house to hang out any chance I got, just to get away from my home situation. Even when Max wasn't there, I would hang out with his younger brother, Kasey. Kasey was a cool kid, and we got along very well. Max and Kasey would argue a lot, but I would always bring them closer together. We would laugh, joke, and have a great time every time we all got together.

During the summer, I also began training for the football season, running hills and miles on the roads by my house. Every morning, I would do hundreds of pushups and sit-ups. Once those were done, I would go to the backyard in the dirt, hot blazing sun and practice throwing the football against objects I would pretend were receivers. I would hike the ball to myself, roll out left and right, and throw at these targets for hours during the day. Sometimes I would practice until the sun went down and it was dark. Although I trained every day, I was skinny and couldn't get bigger for anything. I was in extremely good shape, though. I could run laps around the average person and easily do more pushups and sit-ups than anyone I knew. I was determined to make up for my 8th-grade year when I played football for a team called the Cheetahs in the Junior Midget league and wrestled for the middle school wrestling team. I wasn't too bad at football and didn't win a match in wrestling. My 9th-grade year was not going to be like my 8th-grade year! Every day was hard work in the yard and hard work preparing for the upcoming sports season. It seemed like it was almost like being in prison. I didn't have anything else, so the only thing I could hold on to for hope was my music and sports. I would put on some good music from Bell Biv Devoe, Bobby Brown, Ice Cube, Compton's Most Wanted, DJ Quick, Eazy-E, MC Hammer, and whoever else was hot at the time. It helped me relax and focus on what I needed to do. Listening to BBD helped raise my confidence to talk to that girl I had my eye on in school. I was always a shy kid and would have to work up my confidence to talk to any girl I was interested in. Even late at night, I remember laying on my mattress in my dark room with blankets up where the door was supposed to be for privacy, dreaming about the girl I had a crush on. I would put on some Boyz II Men, Johnny Gill, and Keith Sweat while I lay there thinking about how I could go about asking this girl to go out with me. Who would want to go out with me anyway? I lived in a messed-up house and didn't even have electricity. I would keep myself clean, although I would have to boil a pot of water on the stove to be able to take a bath. I didn't have the latest fashionable clothes or Jordans on my feet, but somehow I managed to keep my appearance up and in style with what I had. Even with the red turtle neck, gold chain, and 1-strapped overalls, I was fresh at my school! That was in 8th grade, though, and they say high school was much different.

This summer, we met another African American family with two boys and two girls around my age. I was excited, and once we met, we all got along and seemed inseparable. This family stayed on the southeast side of Tucson, which wasn't too bad but still had a lot of Blood gangs during this time. My new friends had some of the weirdest names I have ever heard, and their dad was really into black power stuff. Laquita was the oldest. She was about a year older than me. She was cute and knew it, which didn't help anything, but she also had that split personality to the point where she could have a mean streak and didn't want to be bothered by anyone. Kenji was my age. He was the oldest boy in their family. We liked the same music, artists, and sports, and we also liked break dancing. Kenji was a cool dude, but he was a follower and was easy to persuade. Kenji just wanted to always fit in. Djomo was the other boy. He was about a year younger than Kenji and me. Djomo was nice, but he was a huge whiner and was always willing to snitch on everything Kenji and I would do or at least have planned. Kenji and Djomo were always fighting one minute, but they were the best of brothers the next. Djomo was always cool with me and would always hang by my side. It seemed like I was the one to keep Kenji and Djomo from killing each other. Sister was the youngest of us all. She was about two years younger than me. She was more of the quiet type and stuck to herself. I remember her being very helpful and always looking out for everyone, but in the same way Kenji and Djomo were towards each other, Sister and Laquita were identical. They often fought over the littlest things and wouldn't talk to each other for days. Of course, their dad met Joe by coming to the house and doing a drug deal with some weed, but I was grateful for it because now, every time they came down to the house, I would hang out with my new friends. When it was time for them to leave, I would pack and leave with them for the weekend. Sometimes it would be for a couple of weeks! When I hung out with Kenji and Djomo, we never really got into too much trouble, but there were a few times we got into fights with some Crips that stayed a few blocks away. We weren't any hardcore gangbangers, but we formed our own little clique within this Blood neighborhood and would always represent the Bloods even when we weren't one. They were all cool with us, although we didn't participate in many of their activities due to having to be at Kenji's house most of the day. Kenji's mom and dad wouldn't let us hang out in the neighborhood too often.

When we were at the house, his dad would always call me into his room and talk with me about random things and sometimes my future goals. He was a really cool guy. His name was Charles. He was retired from the Army. For some reason, he had his own room, and his wife was in another room all the time. She always cooked and made sure he ate, but I never saw them together unless we all loaded up in the van and went somewhere. I remember the bench press in his room, and I always went into his room and worked out when I got bored with Kenji and Djomo. He would always tell me, "Man! You've got some good traps on you, son." I would always look in the mirror and smile. I wasn't used to compliments, so when I got one on my traps, that only boosted my confidence to walk around with my shirt off around Laquita. When I wasn't hanging out with Kenji and things started to get boring, I would try to work my way in with Laquita. I was attracted to her, and I think she liked me as well, but for some reason, we could never quite hit it off. The farthest I got with Laquita was a 1-minute French kiss because she lost a bet when we played Truth or Dare. That was a great day for a young boy like myself. It wasn't every day that I got to kiss a pretty young girl. Other than this moment, it was very hard to get with Laquita. She wasn't at the age where she was really into boys yet. She was very picky and was disgusted by even a kiss in a movie. It was cool, though. It wasn't like I saw her every day anyway. I would only get to see her a few times a year, mostly in the summer. When we weren't writing songs, wrestling, and doing normal boy stuff, we would create dance routines to perform for their mom and dad. It was fun and brought out the creativity in us. It was awesome to see the smiles on their mom and dad's faces when we performed. It was great to bring them together when we could. As summer started winding down, it was time for me to head back home. This summer would be the last time I would see Kenji, Djomo, Laquita, and Sister for a couple of years.

CHAPTER 5

So It Begins

MY MOM AND Joe picked me up, and we headed back home. I wasn't looking forward to returning home, filling up a generator for lights and electricity, and pouring a pot in the toilet so it could flush. I wasn't looking forward to boiling water on the stove to take a hot bath out of a big pot. I wasn't looking forward to the hard cemented ground with no carpet, and I definitely was not looking forward to not having any walls or privacy with a small narrow blanket up for a door to my room. I kept thinking positively and told myself that I only had a few more days left until the first day of school. This was the only reason I liked going to school so I could get away from home. I thought to myself, "Hang in there. You can do it." It was only for a few more days.

This year is going to be different. This year is going to be awesome! Tossing and turning, I couldn't sleep at night, waiting for school to start the next day. I would have my outfit laid out on my ironing board, ready. I wanted everyone to see that I was the flyest 9th grader at the school. My school wasn't very big, so everyone knew everyone. The first day of high school came, and I was excited to see all of my friends I hadn't seen all summer. Not only my friends, but I would get to see Cecilia, the girl I had a crush on my whole 8th grade year, although she would be going into 8th grade. Cecilia was beautiful. She was light brown-skinned, Hispanic, with black hair, black eyes, and a cute dimple every time she smiled. She finally broke up with her boyfriend, Robbie, and this may be my opportunity to make my move. I saw her on the first day of school, but my shyness kept me from speaking to her. All I could do was smile and say "hi" when I saw her passing. She would be with her friends. Her best friend, Laura, always told me to talk to her. I never would, but I would smile and say hello. That didn't get me anywhere with her.

Classes weren't that bad, but it was a definite change from 8th grade. We were expected to be more responsible and complete our assignments on time with minimal guidance. How could I get all this work done when I had to play sports and write my songs? I was not sure this would work like it did in 8th grade. As I could see already, 9th grade was going to be a challenge. However, I was always ready for a challenge. The only class I seemed to do well in was P.E. I mastered this class! I didn't fail any other classes because I had to play sports and didn't want to be ineligible. I also wasn't a straight-A or B student either. I did just enough to get by, which kept me out of trouble at home and with the coaches. Football season was always at the beginning of the year, and this year I was trying out for QB because I trained all summer and threw my football through the tire I built in the backyard at least 1,000 times. I also threw it probably 50,000 times to the imaginary receivers I had made up in the backyard. I just knew I was ready. The only thing I did not consider was that I would have to compete with some of the other kids that have grown up in this town their whole lives. One of these kids' names was Andrew. He was medium-built and quick. Andrew was one of our school's top athletes. Of course, he was trying out for QB as well. He played QB in Pop Warner, and the coaches were already looking for him to get to high school. It was like I didn't even have a chance to make the starting QB slot.

After summer tryouts, the coaches posted the starting freshman roster, and I didn't make it as the starting QB. I played a bit of wide receiver, corner, and safety during the season. Being new to this school, it was hard to get my foot in the door because all of these kids grew up together, and everyone knew who was already good at each position. It was OK, though. My body was still trying to catch up to my feet. I didn't even have cleats because we couldn't afford them. I had to wear my big white Pony pump-up shoes to every game. I definitely stood out. During one game, I was running down the sideline, and my shoes were so big that one of them flew right off my feet about 15 yards down the field. It was embarrassing, but I didn't let it keep me down or distract me from trying my best and being the best athlete I could be then. I have faced rougher situations in my life, and this was merely another obstacle to overcome. Although I didn't have the latest trends and fashionable clothes, all of the juniors and seniors seemed to like me and always looked out for me. They would ask me to rap and always supported me every time I had a new song to let them hear. After football practice, I would always have to catch a ride home because my parents didn't have the gas money to pick me up. Sometimes I didn't know how I would get home. If Max wasn't there, I would hang out at another friend's house, which was right behind the school. His name was Jorge. He was a short guy, but he had the biggest heart and never quit or gave up. He always gave 100 percent in everything he did. Sometimes, his mom would cook and let me eat with him when I came to his house. If Jorge or Max couldn't take me home, I would sometimes hitchhike and catch a ride home from strangers I didn't even know. I didn't realize how dangerous this could be at the time. My only focus was on getting back home before it got too late. When my friends would drop me off, I would never let them drop me off at my actual house, but at the corner store about a few blocks away. I would make an excuse about having to go by the store first to get something for my parents and that they were meeting me there in a few minutes. I was ashamed to let anyone see the unbuilt house I was living in because you could literally see through the entire house and walls. I didn't want anyone to see these conditions I was living in and go back and tell everyone at school about my circumstances. After all, this was the 1990s, and it was rare to see people living like how I lived.

Every time I would get home, if Joe and my mom weren't working in the yard or on the house, they were smoking weed and doing other drugs with some of their friends that would come over. One of the good things about all of this was that they didn't drink alcohol. I guess there's always some good in every bad situation, right? When I got home, I would go straight to my room, put my headphones on, and work on my music. I would write for hours until I got hungry and needed a break. If my mom wasn't making tortillas and Spanish rice, I would have to make my dinner, boxed macaroni and cheese or Ramen noodles. If I felt creative, I would make Ramen noodles with green beans or corn mixed in it for more flavor. After eating, I would go back to my room, put my headphones back on, and daydream of being with Cecilia one day until I finally fell asleep. As the morning came, it was the same routine each day. I would boil some water on the stove to make sure I had hot water to wash my face and body parts, make sure my hair was combed just right, get dressed, eat a bowl of cornflakes or, if I was lucky, some Quaker oatmeal, brush my teeth, grab my book bag and head to the bus stop. I would see Laura at the bus stop every day, and we would talk about anything worth conversing about. She would always mention Cecilia to me and for me to talk to her. I told her I would someday, but in the back of my mind, I knew I was too shy. Our bus rides were always great conversations and something I looked forward to. Once we got to school, it was the same old thing. The teachers wanted us to do a lot of work in class; riding to G & F pizza or Burger King for lunch; and football practice after school. I always looked forward to the days we had P.E. This was the only class I was really good in.

One of the highlights of my freshman year was our Social Studies teacher knocking on the window of the classroom. The other students and I were puzzled when we saw him staggering and knocking on the window. We laughed, but we opened the window, and he crawled in, staggered to his desk, put his head down, and went to sleep. We couldn't believe that this teacher was drunk and trying to avoid the principal from seeing him come to work late. This was also one of my favorite classes because, surprisingly, we didn't have much work to do. This same teacher was kind of wild as well. I remember hearing about him going on a sports trip out of town. He had some students watching pornography movies and drinking with him in the motel room. I'm not sure what happened to this guy, but he didn't last long at our school. After the weekend football games, we would all get together, party, and drink out in the middle of nowhere with the juniors and seniors. This was where everything went down: fights, sex, alcohol, and drugs. This definitely wasn't middle school anymore. Most people would hook up out there, and you would see them hugged up at school the following Monday morning. It was a great time, especially going to house parties later in the evening. A lot of things took place at these house parties, and it seemed like kids lived for those moments. I wanted to hurry up and be a junior or senior because it seemed like they got all the fine girls and had the most fun. I still kind of fit in, but at the same time, I didn't do a lot of things other kids were doing, such as drugs. I always promised myself I wouldn't be like my parents, and I wanted to succeed in life. If I got involved with drugs, this would definitely ruin my life and possibly shatter my hopes and dreams of becoming something one day.

Some of my favorite moments weren't even at these parties, but the times when Cecilia would stay over at Laura's house for the weekend. I would go over there late at night, and they would sneak out to see me. We would hang out and talk until the early hours of the morning. We were so excited to see each other that time seemed to go by so fast as we talked the night away. Once the sun started rising, Laura and Cecilia would have to return home and sneak back into their room. We would always try to dodge the sensor movement lights that would come on whenever something or someone moved. Once we got past the lights, we were good to go. One particular night, I was brave enough to finally make a move on Cecilia, and we ended up kissing and holding each other all night. This was the beginning of my first relationship and real crush. I would sleep early every night just so the morning would come quicker, and I could see Cecilia for a total of 1 hour at school. During holidays such as Valentine's Day and her birthday, I would go all out by getting the best and biggest balloons, teddy bears, candies, chocolates, and the best Minnie and Mickey Mouse gifts I could find because she loved them more than anything, besides me, of course. I would send the gifts to her class. I was always known for treating her exceptionally well. She loved all of her gifts, and we loved every moment we spent with each other, no matter how brief the time was.

Her parents were not into her dating at all, so seeing each other was a challenge. The other challenge was her being Mexican and me being black. Her dad wasn't too fond of her dating, especially dating a black guy. This caused us to try to sneak around every chance we got. On the weekends when she wasn't at Laura's house, I would have Andrew, Brian, Stevie, Max, Anthony, or whoever else I was hanging out with that night drop me off close to her house. Her parents owned a small store next to her house, and I would dodge her motion sensor spotlight and knock on her window. She would always look surprised to see me, open the window and let me in. She would tell me to be very quiet. We couldn't even really talk because her parents were always up late at night, and sometimes they would come into her room but never see me under the covers with her. We were some brave souls. We were in love, which eventually led to us having our first sexual encounter together. We were both virgins, at least for the most part. This was the first time we both experienced real intercourse. It seemed like this would go on every weekend. She had a huge argument with her parents about not being able to see me, and they invited me over so we could meet. They asked me about myself, my parents, sports, food, and my favorite activities. We talked for a few hours, and finally, they seemed to like me. Now I would come over on the weekends and watch a movie with her mom and dad in the living room with us. Her mom was nice, but her dad, on the other hand, was nice some days, but other days, it didn't seem like he wanted anything to do with me. It was alright because we were in love, and nothing could separate us.

When we weren't together, it was time for sports. Our football team went undefeated my freshman year, and we were expected to be something serious in the future. The next sport I would begin with was wrestling. I was already in really good shape, so the practices were not as tough for me, but our school's wrestling team was always in phenomenal shape and known throughout the state as one of the best programs. Coach Comaduran and Coach Nick were pretty awesome. They were very encouraging and always showed a lot of attention and love to the kids on the team. Unfortunately, I needed a lot of encouragement and love because I had to wrestle Danny Barney, a sophomore, to make the varsity team. This guy was born into a wrestling family, and he would kill me at every practice. I would continue wrestling at the freshman meets. However, I didn't win a single match during my freshman year. This was my first time wrestling, and I had a lot to learn. Coach Comaduran and Coach Nick always encouraged me and told me not to quit. They said one day I would be a great wrestler and to hang in there. They told me to work hard and practice like it was a real meet. I took their advice and continued practicing as hard as I could. Although I didn't win a single meet, I was encouraged and looked forward to next year's season.

CHAPTER 6

Letting Go and Moving Up

TOWARD THE END of the school year, I can remember a specific day when Cecilia came to school crying. Cecilia and Laura told me they needed to speak with me at lunch, and it couldn't wait. I had no clue what was happening, but whatever it was, it was bad enough to the point where Cecilia couldn't go to class because she was crying and seemed very torn. I couldn't imagine what was going on with her, and my heart started racing with anxiety. I told her we could meet at lunch and talk about whatever was going on with her. During lunch, we met and sat in one of our friends' cars so we could have some privacy. Once she looked at me with the pain in her big brown eyes, I could tell she was trying to figure out how she could begin to talk to me. I was worried that maybe she would break up with me. This was my first crush and love. I could not imagine losing her. That was not the case. As she looked at me with pain in her eyes and tears slowly coming down her face, Cecilia told me that she thought she was pregnant. My heart started pounding fast, and my head started sweating. How could she tell her parents something like this? We were both shocked and didn't have any idea what we were going to do. I was only a freshman in high school, and she was in 8th grade. We didn't have a clue about raising a kid.

We were only kids ourselves. How in the world could we raise a child? How would we explain this to her parents when they were already skeptical about me dating their daughter? They were beginning to trust and believe in me.

We were both so worried and didn't know what to do that it caused us to have more arguments. We wouldn't speak to each other for 4-5 days at a time. Cecilia went to the doctor and got a pregnancy test done. We held each other, anxious about the result. I told her not to worry. No matter the outcome, I would always be by her side. The doctor returned with the results in his hand, and as we waited for the actual answer, it seemed like the world was moving in slow motion. He told us that Cecilia was not pregnant. It was a huge relief for both of us when we found out that she wasn't pregnant. We found out some good news, and it was like we had a second chance in our relationship to do things right. Although we got good news, it also seemed like it drove Cecilia and me further apart over time. It was probably because of the real-life scare that could have changed both of our lives forever. It seemed as if we had finally woken up from our fantasyland. Things didn't seem the same, and I think the experience pushed us apart more than it brought us closer together.

We were heading into the summer, and school was getting ready to end. Cecilia and I were still together, but it didn't seem like it. One of the reasons is that Cecilia finally told her parents about us and what had almost happened. Her dad was furious and said he never wanted to see me again. Any relationship in which you can't talk or see each other will drive a wedge between the couple, especially if you are 15 years old and your sex drive is through the roof.

Once summer hit, it was time to get back on the grind, working out and partying with my friends any chance I got. I would also do odd and end jobs around my neighborhood to earn money, such as cutting grass, raking dirt, and washing cars. One man, named Mr. Sam, who lived on the hill, was a retired black guy from the Air Force who would always let me cut his grass and earn extra spending money. I spent a lot of time working at Mr. Sam's house during the summer. One hot Arizona summer day, I was sitting in the living room with my shirt off at my house. As I took a drink from my cold soda, Joe's friend, girlfriend, and their daughter came walking into the house. This was the first time I had ever seen them. I was stunned because their daughter was very attractive and seemed to be very nice and friendly. After all, Cecilia and I seemed pretty much done with each other, although it wasn't official. I hadn't spoken with her in over a month, and I didn't know where we stood in our relationship. I asked her name, and she said, "Monique." I told her my name, and we began to talk. Monique always smiled, and I could tell we were very attracted to each other from the first time we saw one another. She was Hispanic, slim, had a nice figure, with long brown hair, big pretty brown puppy dog eyes, and a smile with a dimple that lit up the entire room. My mom, Joe, and her parents went to do their drug deal and get some weed. They told us they would be back and left us in the house together. At first, we were shy. After all, there wasn't much to do at my house, especially in its current condition. We made small talk and seemed to enjoy each other's company. Although we didn't know each other, we laughed, had a great time, and bonded well. It seemed like time had gone by really fast because before we knew it, everyone came back to the house, and it was time for Monique to leave.

This was also around the same time my sister Delia (DJ) was born. I often had to watch her and ensure she was taken care of if my parents had to handle their business. My sister was awesome and brought me much joy because now I had a baby sister in the family.

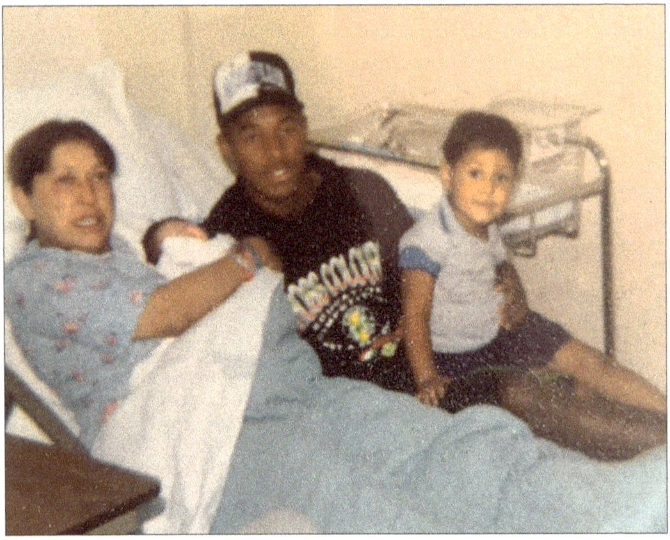

I could now have company to help me when I had to watch her or my little brother. I found out that Monique stayed about half a mile down the road from my house. This is where she would stay for the summer. She stayed with her biological mom, but when the summer was over, she would return to Glendale, which is right outside Phoenix. This is where she lived with her biological dad and stepmom during the school year. My thoughts were no longer about hanging out with my friends for the summer but rather training for the upcoming sports season and the next time I would see Monique. She would begin to come over often because my mom would always ask her to babysit my little brother and sister. Eventually, we started hanging out almost every day for the rest of the summer. We would go to the corner store and get candy, sodas, and our favorite butter crumb cake. We would walk around the neighborhood and talk about anything that came to our minds and what we planned on doing when we got older. We often didn't want to leave each other's company, so she would stay over longer, watch movies late at night, and just chill, talking about our future hopes and dreams. Sometimes she would end up just staying the night. She told me about her parents' situation and why she lived in Phoenix with her dad. She also hated her parents for doing drugs and living the lifestyle of drug dealers, as she never knew what might happen to her or them. We connected on many levels and shared similar experiences, which brought us closer. She also spoke about her current boyfriend and how they were not getting along because he treated her badly and flirted with other girls. They dated for almost three years. Since she shared about her boyfriend, I told her about Cecilia and what happened with our relationship. She advised me not to give up and that we were just going through a rough time, but once I met Monique, it seemed like all of my feelings for Cecilia went away. After all, I didn't deserve to suffer and put myself in a painful situation for someone I could never see for more than an hour a day at lunch. We connected and became best friends. Even though we didn't admit it at the time, in reality, we started falling in love. As the summer was beginning to end, that dreadful day came when it was time for Monique to return home to Phoenix. I remember she just put her head on my shoulder on her last day and cried because she didn't want to leave. We had formed a strong bond, and now it was about to be broken. It seemed like nothing was ever stable in my life, and anytime I let my guard down, whatever it was that meant so much to me would rip my heart out of my chest. I know it wasn't her fault that she had to leave, but I knew I would deeply miss her. Before she left, we exchanged information in hopes of keeping in contact with each other throughout the year. To keep my mind off her as much as possible, I began training more each day until the summer passing league started.

The summer passing league was a high school flag football program concentrating on all skill positions. This helped us prepare for the upcoming season by going over passing drills and practicing pass plays to implement during the regular season. Fortunately, my puberty season was over, and my body was finally coming into alignment, especially my big feet. I felt stronger, faster, and better than I did during my freshman year. I was ready. I had no choice. I had to either play sports, get caught up in activities with some of the local gangs, or be around the daily drug deals going on in and out of my house. I chose wisely and decided to keep going and keep going hard, hoping to play in college and the NFL one day. If that didn't work, maybe I could become a professional wrestler. Speaking of wrestling, this was a huge pastime for me. I had a small TV in my room, and it was all I would watch late at night, daydreaming about being on that stage one day. I would watch it until I couldn't watch it anymore, and the American flag went across the TV screen with the national anthem. This meant that if you didn't have cable, your TV-watching time was done for a few hours, or at least until the early morning. When the TV cut off, I would grab my notebook and headphones and drift off into my songwriting mode, trying to be as creative as possible in hopes of showing off my new songs during the first week of school. Nothing could separate me from writing my music and playing sports. It was like it was meant for me to do this. Although I didn't have power when the generator cut off, I had my flashlight, Walkman, tape recorder, and a lot of batteries because they would die often. Once I was done writing a song, I would get excited about recording it. I had the instrumental tape which would play from one side of the boombox, and the other tape would be for recording. I had a wired mic that ran from the front bottom left side. I would simultaneously hit the play and record buttons, so the blank tape would begin recording. Next, I would push play on the instrumental so the beat would come on. It was like I was in heaven because now I could hear my voice over the beats of the songs, and to me, it was awesome! I would practice hundreds of times on one song until I got it right. Once it was perfected, I would work on a new song. I would continue this entire process until I had both sides of the blank tape filled up. This would give Max and I a lot of music to listen to on the way to school!

CHAPTER 7
The Improvement

MY ALARM CLOCK'S annoying sound was screeching in my ear, and it was time for me to get up. It was a new beginning, the first day of my sophomore year. The temperature was about 100+ degrees in August. I had been working out all summer, so this was a perfect time for me to wear my tank top and Cross Color shorts. I got dressed, and this year was a little different because Max had a car now. He came and picked me up at the house with the stereo blasting. We were no longer freshmen. We felt we had a little more clout now and were looking forward to being able to pick on some of these new freshmen the same way we got picked on last year. Many people said this would be the most boring year of all of high school, but I was bound to make this one of my best years ever.

As we headed to school in Max's Ford Bronco, we had the music turned up. Ice Cube blasted through the speakers as we pulled into the school parking lot. We had more confidence as we now knew what to expect on our first day, unlike last year. Once I stepped out of the vehicle with the hot, blazing sun beaming on my skin, sunglasses on my face, muscles looking nice, and my smooth Cross Colors shorts on, one thought came to my mind immediately. I hadn't seen or heard from Cecilia since a couple of weeks after we left school. She would be a freshman this year, which meant I would see her a lot more now. Previously, she was in 8th grade, which was connected to our high school, and I would only see her around lunchtime and every so often, passing by the other side of the classrooms. I almost completely forgot about her. Was she going to be excited to see me? This was going to be an awkward moment for both of us, but I decided to worry about that when the time came.

It was the first week of school, and as I had been training all summer, my hard work was finally starting to pay off. All the coaches recognized my athleticism and skills that were beginning to come to fruition. They noticed I had gained more muscles and had become more serious than I was in my freshman year. Tryouts began during the passing league of that summer. We would practice in the summer, and now the first week of school would determine our fate to see who made the cut. Whoever made it would be dressing out and playing on Thursday before the varsity game. The roster was posted, and everyone was anxiously looking at the lineup chart to see if their name was listed. I was towards the back and noticed some people walking away with their heads down. As much as I practiced all summer, there was no way I could not make this team. I got closer to the list, looked towards the top and saw my name "Jason Mitchell" right next to the QB position! I made the starting QB spot for the JV team. I was excited but also felt kind of bad because my best friend Max had also tried out for QB. Although he didn't make the starting spot, he was listed as the backup. We've been best friends for a couple of years now, and how would this impact our friendship? Fortunately, Max congratulated me and told me that I deserved the starting position.

He was still happy because he made the first string on defense as well as the punter position.

It was a clear, warm Thursday night, and our first game was at home against our rival school. I was doing pretty well, winning 14-0 going into the 2nd quarter. One key moment of the game came when our rivals punted the ball on 4th and 15 from their 40-yard line. The ball hit the ground and bounced down to our 1-yard line. We were backed up against our end zone. Andy Young ran the play in from the sidelines, and I got the call to run a QB sneak. The plan was to give us some breathing room so we could call some of our basic plays and drive down the field like we were doing the entire game. As I went under center, all I could think about was not getting sacked in the end zone and taking a safety. I looked across at the defense, and they were stacked on the line, hungry, with a look in their eyes that showed they were ready to devour me. I barked the cadence, "Down, set, hut, hut, hut!" The ball was snapped. I took a side step back like we were doing a handoff, turned back towards the line and darted up the middle of the formation. I got through the line, sidestepped, and made a linebacker miss the tackle. I proceeded to head up the field to the left sideline with only the safety left in front of me. I thought to myself, "This was my chance!" Was this really happening? As I ran up the sideline, the safety took a wrong angle and miscalculated my speed. This made him miss the tackle. Now I was all alone, sprinting up the sideline with nothing but the end zone and scoreboard in front of me. I could hear the cheers from the crowd erupt into a roar. I was sprinting as fast as possible and felt like I had never run this fast before. I glanced back, and there was nobody close to me. This was it! The 40, 30, 20, 10, touchdown! I remember everyone running to me and picking me up; the coaches were slapping my helmet, and the crowd was cheering louder than I had ever heard. I just ran for a 99-yard touchdown. The rest of the game went very well, and we beat our rival team 1-0. After the game, I felt amazing and couldn't wait to see all my classmates the next day at school so we could talk and brag about the game last night. Once I got to school, it was announced that I had broken the school's longest-rushing touchdown record. I just made history for my school, as nobody else had ever done this before. When I walked to the P.E. locker room to get ready for P.E. towards the end of the day, I saw the varsity coaches in their office. They pointed at me and motioned for me to come to the office. I walked in and slowly closed the door behind me. Coach Driggers and Coach Bearse told me that I had a great game yesterday and that they felt I could be a great player for the program. They told me to get a jersey out of the jersey box for Friday and dress up for the varsity game. What? I was a sophomore, but I was getting to dress up for varsity? I was excited and rambled through the jerseys and picked out #12. This was the number of my favorite player in the NFL, Randall Cunningham, who played QB for the Philadelphia Eagles. Coach Driggers was also the freshman team coach and had me play QB for them on the Tuesday games. This means I would play three games a week. Well, kind of. I would play the freshman game on Tuesday and the JV game on Thursday, and if we were winning, I would go in for the 4th quarter at the end of the varsity game. It didn't matter to me because I was getting to play a lot of football. This only meant that I was getting more practice and getting a lot better.

During school, I would see Cecilia, and we would speak, but it wasn't the same. We would talk and sometimes eat lunch together. It seemed like she wanted to hang out with her girlfriends more during lunch. This didn't help bring me closer to her, but would begin to push me further away. Since I wasn't talking with Cecilia, I would talk with Monique daily. We would be on the phone for hours, laughing and enjoying each other's voices. Sometimes we didn't even say anything and would fall asleep. Soon, she would begin to come down every other weekend from Phoenix. It wasn't like before when it was just the summer months. She had something or someone to give her a reason to want to come to her mom's house more often. We started hanging out more, and I would tell her about how the football games were going and how everything seemed to be beginning to fall into place. She would tell me about how she was cheerleading for her school and that it was one of her dreams to become a professional cheerleader one day. We would always encourage and support each other, and again, it seemed like we were inseparable, even though we would only see each other every other weekend.

I couldn't go on like this anymore and still be Cecilia. One day, I finally got the courage to write Cecilia a letter and tell her everything about Monique. In the letter, I explained my feelings to her and told her that we should break up because nothing was the same anymore. After about 4-5 drafts of the letter, I felt I finally got it right. The hard part would come in the morning when I would need to give it to her. Once I saw her, my palms started sweating, my heart started racing at 100mph, and I was more nervous than I had ever been in my life. How could I break up with my first love, someone I lost my virginity to, someone I cared for so much? As I proceeded to walk in her direction, she smiled and was waiting for me. I got close to her and thought about not giving her the letter, but my thoughts were that our relationship had been over for a long time. We couldn't continue going on like this. It was time to give it to her, and there was no turning back. As I approached her, she reached out and hugged me, followed by a quick kiss. I gently pulled away and told her, "Cecilia, I have been thinking for a while about our relationship, and there is something I need to give you." Her smile turned into a puzzled look, and she extended her hand to take the letter. She asked me if everything was alright, and I told her, "No, actually, it's not." We sat down on the hard brick wall that was lined up with the sidewalk that everyone used to walk to their classes. She opened the letter and began reading it. I saw her pause a few times, look away, and begin reading again. Tears started to flow from her eyes, and she couldn't hold back the tears. She put her head down with her hands over her face, tears falling on the letter, melting the ink away, and asked me how long I had felt like this. I told her it was all summer. I asked her how we could have a relationship when we didn't even speak or see each other the entire summer. I didn't want to waste my high school years going crazy over a girl I could never see or communicate with. Although she was devastated, she told me she understood and didn't know what to do. We tried to think of ways to make it work, but in the end, it simply would not work. Maybe it was for the best? After about an hour, we both stood up. I pulled her close to me, and we gave each other a hug that seemed to last for eternity. It was like everything felt so right again with her in my arms, but in reality, we both knew that this wasn't going to be able to work out. We agreed that we would still be friends and not be mad at each other. We gave our hearts to each other, and it was a first for so many things for us. This was the hardest thing I had ever had to do because I hated seeing a girl cry. Now I was making one cry. Everyone knew us as the cutest couple in the school, so how would her friends handle this? What would my friends say?

It seemed like the longest night that evening, and I was not looking forward to going to school the next day either. After all, we had been together for almost two years, and I couldn't imagine being away from her after everything we went through together. I knew for sure this was the girl I would end up marrying one day. As I was laying in my bed with my headphones on listening to Bell Biv Devoe's hit song at the time, "Smile Again," I was so upset, wondering if I had made the biggest mistake of my life. All the memories we made together, the special moments, special gifts, seeing her face light up, sneaking out of the house to be with each other, and thoughts of holding one another were constantly running through my mind. This was my first love, and now it is officially over.

CHAPTER 8
What's Next?

THE NEXT DAY of school, I was miserable, walking around with my head down, with no care in the world. Did I make the biggest mistake of my life? That is the only question that I could think about. As I was walking, I saw Cecilia walking with Laura by the lockers. Cecilia tried not to look at me. However, Laura gave me the meanest glare I have ever seen her give anyone. This was not a good sign. As I continued walking through campus throughout the day, I would see Cecilia's friends. They would all give me the meanest look and shake their heads. Why were they so mad at me? Why don't they mind their own business? Did they understand everything we were going through? Was our breakup that serious? My friends were also surprised; half of them didn't believe we had broken up. At least it didn't affect our friendships. It did seem like once we broke up, a few people were trying to make a move on Cecilia. One of my good friends from the wrestling team, Mike, was trying to make a move on her and comfort her behind my back. When she didn't fall for him, other guys began to try, but none of it lasted. Sometimes I felt like she would be seen with them just to try to make me jealous on purpose. It worked in the beginning, but the jealousy slowly began to fade, especially when I was talking with

Monique every night. I had other things to worry about, and one, in particular, was preparing for the upcoming wrestling season. I didn't have time to worry about what was happening with her, who was trying to date her, and what her friends thought. I had to worry about winning my first wrestling match because last year, I literally sucked.

As wrestling season began, I was very nervous and didn't even know if I wanted to go through the pain and torture I faced last year. I sucked it up and walked into the first practice. The smell of the mat and last year's sweaty aroma filled the room. This was a new season, and it was time to move forward. As practice began, I was already in really great shape. This time I just wasn't as clumsy as I was last year. I worked hard on my strength and techniques to get in the best cardio-physical condition possible. I went as hard as I could at every practice for the entire duration. Sometimes I even stayed after practice to work on extra techniques that would help me in the future. Before practice would start each day, we would run for miles through the hot desert sun in the washes filled with soft sand, wearing layers of sweatshirts and sweatpants to lose the excess weight we may have gained. I would always come back either first or, if it was a bad day, at least within the top three. I knew I was beginning to improve, and it was time for me to prove it. The day came when it was time to challenge for the varsity position. Challenges were very important because they would determine who was in the top position in their weight class. A Challenge means you would wrestle other contenders in your weight class for the top spot. My weight class consisted of five people. Of course, I had Danny Barney, who took state last year and was now a junior this year. As the challenges began, I was doing very well and would defeat the other three people in my weight class. Next up was the main event between myself and Danny. The only things I could think of were to be smart and wrestle hard. This guy wasn't built or muscular, but his techniques and skills were ridiculously great. That's all you need to succeed in this sport. As we took our spot in the center of the mat, all the other teammates formed a circle around us. My heart was pounding, and my palms were sweaty. How would I do this time? Was this my chance to make a complete 180 and redeem myself from last year? Could I beat the state champion? All these thoughts raced through my mind as we shook hands and the whistle blew. As we started tugging back and forth, I shocked myself because I could get a good grasp on Danny and take him down to the mat. The first points were mine! "I think this is it. I can do this. I can beat this guy." This was easier than I thought. I was not going to be intimated any longer. As I was working my skills and technique moves against him on the mat, the whistle blew, and the end of the 1st period was over. I wasn't tired yet, but I saw him breathing a little heavier than I was used to seeing him. This was a great sign for me because, at that moment, I knew I was in better shape than he was. The beginning of the 2nd quarter began, and once again, we were tugging back and forth. This time, the circumstances turned out different. My confidence made me make a dumb mistake, which Danny took full advantage of. The next thing I knew, I was down on the mat, trying to work my way out of his grip, which wasn't happening. He scored his 2 points by taking me down and continuing to apply moves he had mastered over the years. This guy had been wrestling since he was 4 years old and came from a long lineage of wrestlers. I was beginning to get tired, which enabled him to get on my back. I had about 20 seconds left until the buzzer sounded and I could get a fresh start. I kept thinking to myself to hold on, hold on! The buzzer sounded. I didn't get pinned, but now I was down by 3 points. I felt like I had crashed into a brick wall because I was winded and my body had just shut down. It seemed like Danny had caught a second wind, and we still had another period to go. The 3rd period begins, and Danny immediately takes me down, scoring more points. At that moment, I knew it was over for me. His techniques and skills were too much for me to overcome, and I was too tired to attempt a comeback. Danny pinned me at about a minute left in the match, and I was eliminated from JV while he advanced to varsity as expected.

Although I was not on varsity, I noticed that I had drastically improved my skills, techniques, and strengths. At least I was second for varsity if he ever got hurt and first position for JV. I could only get better as long as I could hang in there and not give up.

The first day came for our JV wrestling invitational, and it was a cold December night. This was my first real match of the year. I haven't had a match since all of the matches I lost my freshman year. When I look back, I can't believe I didn't win a single match that year. Was I really that bad? On the day of our first meet, we traveled to the school where the invitational would take place for about an hour. I had trained hard and felt as ready as I could be. After all, I had been wrestling the state champion in practice every day and was improving. In the locker room, when I was changing, all I could think about was staying smart, using my strength and applying everything I learned. This year was going to be different, and there was no other option. Once the invitational started, we watched match after match, and all of our teammates dominated their weight class. I didn't want to be the guy to mess up the roll our team was on. My weight class was called, and I went to the mat where I would be wrestling. I was in the hole, warming up and nervous as could be. When you were in the hole, you were next up after the current match was over. Jimmy Rivera was on the mat at the time, and this guy was also destined to be a state champion. He took the mat, the whistle blew, I turned around for 5 seconds to tie my shoes, and the match was over! Jimmy pinned his opponent in 30 seconds. This guy was a beast! I wasn't expecting to be up so quickly. I took my warm-up gear off and stepped onto the mat for the first time this season. Focused and determined to get my first victory, I was ready for my opponent. As the whistle blew, I immediately took the guy down and began to work the techniques I had learned from Danny on him. I turned him over and almost pinned him in the first round, but somehow he managed to escape the buzzer. My coach told me, "You've got this. This is what you have been training for all year and working so hard in practice for. Go out there and pin this guy!" Once the 2nd round began, he took me down, and memories and thoughts of my losses started coming back into my mind. He started to turn me over but over-applied himself, which threw him off balance. I was able to counter his move, flip him over, and put him on his back. I held on and squeezed as hard as I could. I don't think I ever squeezed anything as tight as I was squeezing him as his back was flat on the mat. I felt him beginning to give up, and all I could see was my coach screaming and jumping up and down. The next thing I knew, the referee's hand hit the mat, and the whistle blew, which only meant this guy just got pinned! I was so excited I didn't know what to do. This was my first match of the year, and I just won! As we continued through the invitational, I would continue to win my matches and move up the bracket. I went to the bracket to see who my next opponent would be, and it was a guy from Bisbee named Eli. This guy was similar to Jimmy but not as strong, and he was a little more beatable. As we took the mat, this would determine who would go to the finals to wrestle for first and second place. I was focused, on a roll, and felt unstoppable at the time. Unfortunately, as soon as the referee blew the whistle, Eli commenced to take me straight to the mat. Once this happened, I knew it would be a long match. He continued to work his skills on me and almost pinned me until I was smart enough to keep getting out of bounds. If it weren't for the out-of-bounds lines, I would have been done in the 1st period. As the 3rd period began, Eli's strength proved too much for me as he took me down again and again until he finally got me on my back in the middle of the mat. There was no escaping his strong grip this time, and instead of me getting the victory, it was Eli as the referee's hand hit the mat, and the whistle blew out loudly. I lost the match, but I wasn't as disappointed as I thought I would be because I knew I was much better than I was last year. I knew I was going to be a problem for these guys very soon. During the finals, Eli and Jimmy wrestled each other, which ended with Jimmy pinning Eli in the 2nd period for the championship. This guy was unstoppable and a force to be reckoned with this year. How was anyone going to defeat this guy? I guess we will find out soon enough.

Wrestling season was coming to an end, and throughout the year, I was able to redeem myself from the previous year. I lost nine matches, mostly to Eli and Jimmy throughout the season, but I won fourteen. That was a big improvement from 0 in my freshman year. I beat all my other opponents and needed to figure out a way to beat Jimmy and Eli next season. Jimmy went undefeated for the 2nd year in a row, winning the state championship as a sophomore. Eli would take second with his only loss to Jimmy. This was going to be interesting over the next two years as we were all in the same weight class.

CHAPTER 9
Another Year

AS THE YEAR was coming to an end, I met another girl named Monica at a party on Saturday night. Monica was good at basketball and was expected to transfer to my school next year. She was a little taller than me, with an athletic body, nice legs, dirty blonde hair, and blue eyes. She definitely got my attention. Devon was hosting a party at her house, and a lot of my classmates and athletes were planning to attend. Devon was short, Hispanic, cool, and had a lot of freedom to do whatever she wanted. Her parents were down-to-earth people and let her have sleepovers and parties all the time with both boys and girls. Her place was the place to be. Devon was dating a junior named Gabe. Gabe was Hispanic, 5'9," 175 lbs, medium build, black hair, and had one eye that was a little crooked, which gave him a crazy look. Gabe was known as a cool dude, but he also caught up with some wrong people and became involved with gangs in Tucson. He also played sports and had a side that was quick to look out for his homies. Gabe wouldn't take crap from anyone. He was very protective of his sister, Lindsey. He wouldn't start any trouble with anyone, but if there was trouble starting with him, Gabe would find himself in the mix and wasn't scared to help end it quickly.

As the summer approached, this was the first time I started drinking continuously and sneaking out of my house to go to parties. I was sneaking out way more than I was during the previous summers. I wasn't with Cecilia anymore, and I didn't hear much from Monique often, so I didn't think too much about our relationship. I was single, free, and ready to run through as many girls as possible, as I had lost feelings for girls. I was sick of being hurt and didn't want to be hurt any longer. This time, I was going to be the one doing the hurting. Once I started hanging out at some of the parties, it seemed like Gabe and I were beginning to get closer, and we became friends. We would always get each other beers and talk about girls. We would mention who we wanted to get with next and sometimes even place bets on who would get with whom we bet on first. When I didn't have a ride home, Gabe would always welcome me to stay at his house. Of course, I would accept because I definitely wasn't going home with alcohol on my breath. Plus, it gave me more freedom and time to chase some of the girls I would meet. Gabe also had a lot of freedom, and whatever we wanted to do, we would do it. His mother, Rosemary, was Hispanic, of slender build, with black hair and small freckles. She was very welcoming. Rosemary became like my second mother, and she would always make sure I had anything I needed. She had some other teens she took in as well, Eric and Rolando. These guys were also like me in their situations. They had to provide and make way for themselves in order to survive. Rosemary had no issues with looking out for us as her kids. Her husband, Wayne, was a truck driver, and we would see him randomly when he wasn't on the road working. Rosemary always ensured that Gabe and Lindsey were doing well in school and not getting into trouble. If something went down, she wouldn't hesitate to have Gabe or Lindsey's back.

One summer night, a couple of weeks after school ended, I remember being at a random party. We were all drinking and having a good time. As I looked across the way, I saw Monica. Monica was looking back at me. By this time, I was much bolder than I was in my two years of high school. I now had athlete status, was well built, girls thought I was cute, and I was getting more popular in my school. I walked over to Monica and started a conversation with her. I am not quite sure of the details, but I remember we laughed and had a great time. As the night went on, it seemed like everything else disappeared, and it was just Monica and I having a great conversation and enjoying each other's company. She didn't really drink, so I respected that and would only drink enough to keep me comfortable while I was with her at the party. At the end of the night, everyone started to leave, and of course, I wasn't ready to go home. I was beginning to have a good time with Monica. My homeboy, Gabe, was still there and told me he was going to take the party to his Nana's house because she was out of town. He would often watch her house and had the key to the liquor cabinet as well. This was awesome because we could continue drinking, have some privacy, and keep the party going there without anyone bothering us. Since the night was winding down and we were all leaving, I asked Monica if she wanted to come with us. I explained that we wouldn't do anything but hang out, drink, and watch movies. To my surprise, she told me she wanted to come. We all loaded up in the vehicles, and as usual, after the parties, we went to Burger King to get some food. After we had ordered our food, we headed to the house, and Monica followed us. I remember she drove her vehicle. We pulled up, got out of the vehicles, and went into the house. By this time, a lot of things were blurry, and I can remember Monica taking me to the bedroom. We sat and talked on the bed for a while. Before I knew it, we started kissing and making out. We were getting hot and horny and began to take our clothes off. Before it got too heated, I remembered I had no condoms. I told her to hold on. She asked me if something was wrong, and I told her I didn't have any condoms. I said to hold on, don't move, and I would be right back. I put my pants back on and went into the living room to ask Gabe if he had some condoms. He said he didn't have any more at the house but had some back at his mom's house. That was 20 minutes away, which meant it would be at least 40 minutes if we went to get them. By this time, she might have changed her mind. All I could think to myself was that there was no way this could be happening to me. The star female basketball player is lying in bed naked, and I don't have any protection! I came back to the room and told her what had happened. She was still ready to do what we had planned without protection, but I told her I couldn't. We were so young, dumb and horny that we came up with an idea to get some Saran Wrap and use that as a condom. I went to the cabinet to check if there were any, and they were sitting right in front of me. I grabbed it and went back to the bedroom. We wrapped the Saran Wrap around me and began to have intercourse. As much as I wanted it to at that moment, it wasn't working out with the Saran Wrap. We decided to stop and eventually laughed at the entire situation. We still talked and had fun the rest of the night, but other than a couple of other minor encounters at her house, we didn't see each other very often.

Again, summer was upon me, and my focus was on training, writing my songs, and earning money to party and buy the latest fashionable clothes. I was now a cool kid at my school, and I had to have money to look fly for the girls. I was sitting at my house when I heard a knock at the door. I got up to see who it was, and to my surprise, it was Monique! I was excited to see her. Every feeling I had from last summer and the few times I saw her over the weekends immediately came back. We hugged, she came in, and we sat on the sofa. She told me that my mom called her and wanted her to start babysitting DJ this summer. I was excited as this would give us the opportunity to see each other more often when I wasn't at practice. During the summer, I had more training for football with two-a-day practices at the school. We would lift in the morning and do drills and exercises in the afternoon. After practice, I would rush home, sweaty and all, just to see if Monique was at my house or not. Most of the time, she was there watching my sister. We would hang out, talk, and continue where we left off last summer. This time it was very different. Although we had a lot of feelings for each other, I thought she still had a boyfriend in Phoenix. After we talked, she told me she had broken up with her boyfriend and was now single. I didn't care about her old boyfriend as I wanted to be the next man in her life. How could I do this, and how could it work when she lived so far away? As each day passed, we spent countless hours together and finally decided that it was time that we give this relationship a shot. After all, we were best friends, and I broke up with Cecilia over her. She told me she and her boyfriend broke up over me, although they were already on the verge of breaking up. It was like they were in a similar situation as Cecilia and me, but without the pregnancy scare. It seemed like the time was right. Although I was partying and having a great time chasing other girls at parties, malls, movies, and anywhere else Gabe and I could find them, I felt Monique was the only one for me. We began dating seriously over the summer, and it was rare that you would catch us apart. It got to the point where it was so serious that her mom and stepdad asked her if she wanted to move in with them so she could be closer and go to school with me. Of course, she said yes, but her parents in Phoenix weren't fond of the idea of her moving away from them and being with her mother. After all, her mother was into drugs, which was one of the reasons they were not together. I couldn't blame her parents for being so angry and despising the idea, but eventually, they agreed to give her mother a second chance.

As the summer began to wind down and my junior year of high school was rapidly approaching, I had to ensure I was in the best shape possible. I wanted to pick up from where I left off last year. Again, I was getting bigger, stronger, and faster than the previous year. I had to be ready because this was all I had to keep me away from my home and street life. I didn't want to be like Joe and my mom, so I had to hold onto my dreams and work hard to achieve them. The summer heat in Arizona was scorching hot, especially with a helmet and pads on. Although it was hot, we had to push through the heat mentally and continue to train and adapt our bodies for the upcoming season. People would pass out from the conditioning drills. Half of the team would lie on the grass while a few others would throw up at the back of the end zone. I was still in great shape, and the conditioning drills didn't affect me. For some, I guess that partying over the summer weekends didn't help them get ready and in shape for "Hell Week."

CHAPTER 10
Problems

THIS YEAR WAS going to be amazing. After all, my new girlfriend moved all the way from Phoenix to be closer to me and goes to the same school. It was bound to be awesome. As the first day of school approached, I left my house and met Max at the corner store as I usually did, but this time Monique accompanied me. He was surprised as well, as he wasn't expecting to see her. We got to school, and everything was lovely. I was now a junior, which is considered an upperclassman, and everybody knew who I was. They were going to meet my new girlfriend, who they had heard so much about, and who supposedly caused the breakup with Cecilia. Once we got to school, we kissed, hugged, and left each other to attend our classes for the day. As the day progressed, I learned that Cecilia and some of her home girls found out about Monique. They were in the same grade and ended up in some of the same classes. People were talking, and word got around the school that there would be a huge fight! This was only the first day of school, and why was Cecilia trying to fight Monique? Our relationship was over, and we were not seeing each other anymore. It was time for her to move on. I believed her feelings got the best of her when she saw the girl who "stole" me from her. She was determined to get revenge;

the only way to do that was to beat her up. Monique handled herself well, and the fight never took place. However, Cecilia and about five of her friends would constantly harass Monique every chance they got. There wasn't a day that went by without one of Cecilia's friends cussing Monique out. They would also try to instigate a fight with her every chance they got. It was ridiculous and was beginning to get very old. There were many times I would have to step in and tell them to leave her alone. After school, Monique would often cry on my shoulder and second-guess her decision to move here to go to school with me. Although we were boyfriend and girlfriend, most importantly, we were best friends. I was able to talk to her, give her advice, and comfort her as much as possible, ensuring that everything would be OK. I was only a junior in high school. Was I supposed to be going through all of these problems? I didn't have any issues, but it bothered me that my best friend and girlfriend would cry herself to sleep some nights. Eventually, the bullying began to slow down, and life started to return to normal. I could finally concentrate on football without having to worry about if my girlfriend was getting jumped or not.

It was Friday night, and although I didn't make the starting QB position this year, I was starting as a cornerback for our varsity football team. I was the backup QB to our returning senior QB, Lacey Barney. Lacey's brother was Danny Barney, the state champion guy I had to wrestle the last two years. It seemed like I could never get away from these guys. It was alright, though, because our team was picked to go to the state championship game this year. One of the main reasons is that my junior class was undefeated for both our freshman and sophomore years. Now we were moving into the varsity spot behind the senior class. It was going to be an exciting season. As the lights shone brightly on the field, the smell of grass filled the air, cowbells rang out, and the warm weather glistened on our skin. It was time for some football. The banner was up, the cheerleaders were yelling, and the crowd was going crazy as we ran onto the field, smashing through the banner. Our music was playing, we were hyped up, and it was time to go to work. It was time to prove to everyone how good we were because of our hard work this year. We lined up across the field as the start of the game proceeded when the referee blew his whistle. The kickoff sailed to the opponent's 10-yard line with a short run back to the 20-yard line. The crowd was screaming as our senior lineup took the field for the first series on defense. Only three players on defense weren't seniors, and I was blessed to be one of them. We had a hunger in our eyes that I could not explain. On the first snap, the QB took the ball and, not even two seconds later, was crushed in the backfield. Coverage was on point, and there was nowhere to throw the ball. I was excited as I passed the first test by not letting a senior beat me for a pass. As the game went on, we continued to score on offense, and our defense continued to shut everything down that the opposing team would throw at us. They couldn't move the ball against our defense, and once again, we scored another victory. It was an amazing feeling to be able to start on defense, make some key plays and help our team get the victory.

As the season continued, we dominated and got victory after victory. I was able to play very well and had minimum plays thrown in my direction to where I was beat. Our team was headed to the playoffs and on our way to proving we were state champions. In our first playoff game, we dominated the opposing team and won 35-7. I had an interception in the game, and only two passes were caught by the receiver I was covering for minimum gains. We were headed to the semi-finals. If we won this game, we would go to the state championship game as predicted. This game was bound to be a very good game as the opposing team had a great QB and wide receiver duo that dominated their division this year. I was matched up against the wide receiver for this game. The game was scoreless until the 3rd quarter. The receiver I was covering was very quick and only had one reception the whole game for 10 yards. I was lucky because he had me beat a few times, but the QB didn't see him. This time we were matched up in man-to-man coverage, and my coach told me to bump him at the line. Once the ball was hiked, I bumped him, which threw off his timing. However, our feet got tangled up, I fell to the ground, and he ran down the sideline alone. All I could think was, "Please don't throw the ball to him!" Our safety shifted too far to the middle of the field, and the QB launched the ball 40 yards down the field to this receiver. It seemed as if everything had begun to move in slow motion. The receiver reached his arms out for the ball. It bobbled, but he grabbed it and continued to sprint down the sideline for the only score of the game. This was it. Was our season over? All of the work we did this offseason, all of the games we played our butts off for, and now it was coming to a close. The score was 6-0 in favor of the opposing team. We had one last chance to move the ball down the field and score. There was 1 minute left in the game, and it seemed like none of our plays were working. Finally, we started moving the ball down the field and getting first down after first down. There were 30 seconds left in the game, and we were facing a 1st and 10. Lacey dropped back for a pass and threw the ball over the receiver's head for an incomplete pass. 2nd down and 10 to go. Lacey dropped back and threw for a short pass close to the sidelines, but it bounced off the receiver's hands. 3rd down and 10 to go with 15 seconds left on the clock. When Lacey dropped back for a pass, nobody was open, so he started to scramble and took off running. He ran for 35 yards and went out of bounds at the 20-yard line. Now it was 1st down from the 20-yard line with only 5 seconds left on the clock. When Lacey took the snap, it bobbled in his hands, and by the time he could recover the ball, three opposing players were driving him to the ground. There was no more time left on the clock. Our season was officially over.

All the hard work, blood, sweat, and tears went straight down the drain. All we could do was take off our helmets and shoulder pads and drop our heads as we walked off the field after shaking hands with the opposing team. This was it. Our season was over. It was a long bus ride home that evening, but there was still hope for next year. We didn't know what it was like to lose, and the feeling of losing our first game was devastating. We definitely didn't want to feel this again next year, especially having the best players in the state of Arizona on our team. We had one more chance, but that chance seemed like it was a long way away.

We got back to our city and offloaded all of our gear. Although we were feeling down and depressed about the loss, a lot of guys still wanted to celebrate and party because of being able to get as far as we did. Actually, some guys just wanted to make up anything they could to have a reason to party. Even though we were feeling down, this would be the chance to drown our sorrows and reminisce. Later that evening, around midnight, we all got together and met at our usual spot in the middle of nowhere. This was where everyone threw the wildest parties and bonfires, and adults couldn't complain about the music being too loud. Once we got to the spot, a lot of beers were cold and ready, waiting for all of us football players to arrive. Everyone was drinking tonight. Even people that I had never seen drink before had some alcohol in their hands. All of the kids were passing the football players beer after beer so we could drown our sorrows and forget about the loss from earlier that evening. We had a great time reminiscing about the season, both the good and the bad. This made us feel a lot better as we would clown about some of the things that happened throughout the year. We made fun of some of the coaches and how they would yell at certain players. It seemed like the loss hurt us very badly. However, times like this pulled us closer together, and the memories we shared will be forever in our hearts and minds.

Later that evening, as the party was ending, I met up with Gabe, and we planned to return to his Nana's house. Of course, that meant more drinking, but I wasn't thinking of any girls this time because I was dating Monique now. She happened to be at her dad's house in Phoenix this weekend, so I couldn't hang out with her. Gabe was driving an old beat-up van that night. I had no idea where he got this van from, but there were two seats in the front and one row of seats in the back. As we drove home, we decided to stop at 7-11 and get a hot dog. We didn't have any business driving that night as we were both pretty drunk. We pulled into the 7-11 and parked in the parking space crookedly. Luckily, it was late at night, and there weren't many people around. We got our hot dogs, left the store, and returned to the vehicle. We only had a few more blocks before we got to the house. As Gabe made a left turn at an intersection, red and blue lights began to flash behind us. I knew this wasn't going to be anything good.

CHAPTER 11
The Journey Continues

WE BOTH BEGAN to panic, trying to figure out what we would do next. As I saw the cop exit the vehicle and walk towards the driver's side of the van, I slowly opened my door and began to get out. I slowly and softly closed the door and hopped over a small fence right next to the sidewalk. Once I got over the fence, I ran as fast as I could, thinking that the cop had seen me. I fled through about six houses, yards, and fences and ran one mile to this guy named Roo. Roo was our star running back and would often let me come hang out with him when I had no place to go. I got to his house and banged on his window. I told him what had happened and that we needed to try and find out if Gabe was arrested and went to jail. He told me to calm down and said I was crazy for running. I explained to him that I wanted to call and make sure Gabe was alright, but the cops were probably looking for me since I took off running. Roo called down to the police station and asked if there had been someone arrested within the last couple of hours named Gabe. The station told him "no." We were puzzled because he was drunk, and the cop pulled him over. Did Gabe run too?

After a few hours, we decided to drive back down to Nana's house, where Gabe should be if he weren't arrested. We pulled up in the driveway, and the van was parked on the street by the house. Gabe saw us pull up and came out of the house with a bottle of Tequila in his hand, asking if we wanted some. This dude was seriously crazy! I asked him what had happened and how he didn't go to jail. He told me the cop pulled him over because his left tail light was out. When the cop walked up to the van, he shined his flashlight on the other side and asked where the other person in the van went. Gabe said he looked to the right, and I wasn't in the seat, and then he turned around and looked in the back. He was confused but told the cop that there wasn't anyone else in the van and he must have thought he saw someone else. The cop was confused, and after he looked into the van some more, he told Gabe that he needed to get his tail light fixed and to have a good night. After we laughed and clowned for about 30 minutes, it hit me that this dude was my ride-or-die brother. He had a chance to tell the cops that I had run from them, but he didn't. He wasn't a snitch. He always looked out for me and made sure I had money if I needed it, food, and a place to stay. We always had alcohol and chased girls together. This guy was my homie for life, and I would do anything for my new brother.

When we woke up the next morning, on Saturday around 2 pm, Gabe got a call from some of his friends in Tucson who were gangbangers. They told him that they were going to have a huge party that evening with a live DJ, a lot of alcohol, and a lot of girls. Gabe asked me if I wanted to go up there with him. Of course, I said yes, but I needed to change my clothes. He got dressed, and we headed to his mom's house to take the van back and switch into the car with tinted windows. My house was on the way heading towards Tucson, so we stopped there long enough for me to change clothes. Once I got dressed, we hopped back into the car and headed out. On the way to Tucson, he told me I might see some stuff up there that I wouldn't normally see. He said always to watch my surroundings and be careful because these dudes were serious bangers. I agreed and proceeded to open up the tequila bottle we had brought with us. We took about six shots each by the time we arrived at our destination. We pulled up and got out of the car. We were at a white-bricked house that looked kind of old and run-down. There was a chain link fence around the house with a gate to get in. Outside the house, about seven guys were sitting on the steps and in chairs on the porch. Most of them had blue rags on their heads. The ones that weren't wearing them on their heads had them hanging from their back pockets. They had on blue, sagging dickie pants, wife beaters, plain white tee's, and a couple of them had on blue and black patterned flannels. The flannels were partially buttoned, and most of them had on old-school black Nikes with the white Nike stripe down the side. When we walked up, they all nodded and smiled. They gave both of us a dap and seemed really happy to see Gabe. I was an outsider they had never seen before, but luckily they all seemed cool with me since I was with Gabe. There were three guys smoking weed on the porch. They asked me if I wanted a hit. I told them no and that the only thing I did was drink because I was into sports. They were cool with my answer and passed me a Corona, which I gladly accepted.

We all sat around, and they caught up with Gabe since they hadn't seen him for a while. They talked about old times and asked him how he'd been. He caught them up on everything, and they told him they were proud of him. At around 6 pm, it was still light outside, and I guess everyone was starting to get bored. One of the guys suggested we head up to this spot in the middle of nowhere outside Tucson. He told us that there were devil worshippers out there that were doing their rituals and we should go beat them up. Everyone got excited, and the next thing I knew, four guys went inside the house. I didn't know what to expect and was kind of shocked. They came out about two minutes later with about six bats. They said, "Let's go," and we walked to Gabe's car. One guy popped the trunk and put the bats and a cooler filled with alcohol in the trunk. One of the guys was just smoking weed, didn't have any alcohol, and volunteered to drive. As we were all loaded up in the vehicle, I could only imagine what would happen next. I wasn't nervous anymore because the braveness and boldness of these guys also made me feel like we could do anything we wanted. It was like they were fearless and didn't have a care in the world. Plus, we were going to look for these devil worshippers that don't need to be here, right?

As we were riding to where these people were supposed to be, we ended up on a back road. There weren't many cars out there, as we were in the desert area outside Tucson. We had N.W.A. blasting through the radio, drinks in our hands, and were ready to accomplish the mission we set out to do. As we drove down this long road, we heard a siren and red and blue lights flashing behind us. Not again! The Tucson Police Department (TPD) was coming up on us fast. We didn't know what to do, and everybody started shouting to remain calm. As the cop got closer, we pulled over to the side of the road. We had a bag of sunflower seeds, and everyone started shoving them in their mouths to get rid of the alcohol smell on our breath and in the car. The cop walked up to the passenger side window and told the guy in the front seat to roll the window down. He rolled the window down and asked the officer how he was doing. The officer said, "I'm doing fine, but what are y'all boys doing out here?" All I can remember was a lot of stuttering and nervousness from everyone. The officer then asked us to roll down the back window. I was in the back seat, where the window was located. I rolled down the window and had a mouth full of sunflower seeds. The officer asked my name, and I couldn't even talk because of how many seeds were in my mouth. He then opened the door and told me to get out of the vehicle and spit out whatever was in my mouth. I was spitting out sunflower seeds for at least 5 minutes. He told everyone else to step out of the vehicle and spit out whatever they had in their mouths as well. Once we were all out, he made us sit on the side of the road, Indian style, with our legs crossed while he checked the driver's ID. He ran his license through the system, and surprisingly, it came back clean. The driver wasn't drinking, so he issued all of us underage drinking violations and told us that we would have to appear at the Tucson courthouse. Our hearts were racing because we just knew we were going to jail. For some reason, the cop never checked the trunk. If he had, he would have seen the bats and the cooler filled with alcohol. We were blessed to be able to get back in our car. We could have easily been arrested, put in the cop's car, and taken to the TPD station. Needless to say, once we got back in the car, we headed back to the house.

It was a quiet ride back to the house. However, once we pulled up, it was like nothing ever happened. The bottles started popping, and the weed started lighting up again. About 20 minutes later, we were all having a great time and clowning about how the cop had me spitting out the sunflower seeds for 5 minutes. By this time, it was around 9 pm. The sun was down, and other cars started pulling up to the house. People started parking along the road and on both sides of the streets. The

DJ pulled up and unpacked his gear. Everyone who pulled up to the party wore blue, black, and white. There wasn't a sign of red on any of these dudes. It was a mix of Black and Mexican guys and girls. Even the girls were in blue and black. These cats were serious about their colors and represented their Crip affiliation to the fullest. They ranged from the ages of about 16-35. The older guys seemed more relaxed and laid back. Many of the younger cats were too busy trying to show off in front of the girls, trying to impress them, and would talk crap to each other. It was interesting and funny at the same time. For the rest of the night, we drank, ate, and had a good time listening to music and talking about life. The older guys would tell us that there was more to life than gangbanging, and jail wasn't a place we wanted to go. They said there was no hope or future for the people locked up for life in there for the stupid crimes they committed within a split-second decision. They claimed to have a lot of their homies locked up and told us they were blessed to be walking around in freedom. I listened to all of the knowledge they were sharing and was still wondering in my head why they were still representing their Crip gang. They knew the consequences that came with gangbanging.

I didn't get any girls that evening because I was too busy listening to the OGs share their wisdom. I loved being with these guys because it seemed like the family I had never had, and they protected each other to the fullest. The only problem was that I was an athlete and didn't want to throw my hopes and future down the drain by being in the wrong place at the wrong time with these guys. As the night ended and it turned about 4 am, Gabe and I gave dap to the few guys and girls still awake or not hooking up with someone in the bedroom. We told them we had a good time, got back in the car, and headed home. We talked and clowned the whole way home. I told him I had a great time except for the minor incident. I said that the OG's shared a lot of wisdom, and I couldn't understand why the young dudes were still trying to bang. He said it was a lifestyle for them, and most of them grew up in that lifestyle, which was all they knew. It was almost like it was their culture. Most of their relatives were banging, and the ones that weren't banging anymore were either dead or in jail. He agreed that there wasn't any future in that lifestyle, but something about it kept Gabe from completely letting it go.

CHAPTER 12

In The Mix

NOW THAT FOOTBALL season was over, it was time for wrestling season to begin again. Once again, Danny was still wrestling. He was the state champion for the last 3 years and now a senior. He was still in my weight class, but I knew I was much better than my sophomore year. This year I was going all out and planned on being varsity since I had already made the varsity football team. This guy wasn't going to stop me like he did the last 2 years.

We continued with our practices as we would normally do. We ran for miles in the sand and went over techniques, skills, and conditioning for about three weeks before we started challenges. The day finally came for the challenges, and I was ready to beat Danny and take that varsity spot. The coaches called us to the center of the mat, blew the whistle, and we began to grapple. I took Danny down. He immediately escaped and took me down. I would escape and get him back down. This would go on for all three rounds. Danny didn't pin me this time, but he beat me by about 5 points. I was disappointed that I was back on JV, but at the same time, I thought about what had just happened. I may be wrestling for the JV team again this year, but I have been wrestling a state champion for the last 2 going on 3 years. Everyone told me that once I became a senior, I would be really good and probably go undefeated. I was excited, but at the same time, I was tired of wrestling JV while my friends, like Jorge and Brian, were on the varsity team.

As the season went on, I continued to excel and show that I was a force to be reckoned with. I was winning all my matches, and the only competition I had was some wrestlers from schools that we had never really faced except at tournaments. Eli and Jimmy were on the varsity team, so I didn't have to wrestle against them, although they were still in my same weight class. Match after match, I was defeating and pinning opponents within 30 seconds. I was beating opponents by technical points, and the referee was stopping the match. I was killing every opponent that was coming across my path. Although I wasn't on varsity, the varsity and JV teams from other schools knew who I was and that I wasn't a pushover. They knew the only reason I was on JV was that Danny Barney was an excellent wrestler who was a 3-time state champion and was also predicted to win state for the 4th time this year. This was the only reason I was not on that varsity team, and I was set to prove something to the entire wrestling world that crossed my path. This year, I finished the season with a record of 21-2. The two losses that I faced were against some bigger-name schools in Tucson during an invitational meet. Sunnyside was known as one of the top programs in the country, and they were based right there in Tucson. We had an invitational meet in which their school participated, and I lost both matches to the same school. In the first match, I lost 12-9, and in the second, I lost 9-4. These guys were really good wrestlers, and both of them reminded me of Danny Barney's skills. I was proud of my season, but I was even more anxious and ready for next year.

While I was walking to class, one of the track coaches approached me. He asked me if I had ever thought about running track. I told him no and that I wasn't fast, but I was quick. He told me that running track would help me with the other sports I was playing. I thought about it and told him I would give it a try. I didn't know what race I would run because I was new to running track. I went out on the first day, and we began to practice. Coach Jerry would call out the different races, and everyone would fall into that area if they were interested. All I ever heard about or paid attention to was the 100-meter, 200-meter, and 400-meter races. The first race I tried out for was the 100 meters. I did ok, but out of seven people, I came in 4th. I continued to practice for this race, and soon the season began. I remember our first track meet. There were girls everywhere. It seemed they were interested in all the guys winning their races. Once they called the 100-meter participants to head to the starting line, I knew this was my chance to show off and impress the ladies. I took off my jacket and sweatpants and jumped up and down like everyone else seemed to do to warm up their muscles and stretch out. I got in the starting blocks, and the next thing I remember was coming in 4th place again! This would continue for about four more meets until my coach brought me to the side and told me to try out the hurdles. "The hurdles! I ain't never ran hurdles before. What if I fall and scrape up my legs?"

Although I didn't want to, I gave the hurdles a chance. I began to practice daily and started to get addicted to the skill and technique it took to run hurdles. I would stay late after practice and continue trying to perfect my form, which was the key element in this race. You didn't have to be super fast, but if you had great form and decent speed, you could excel in this race. Although the season was coming to an end, I had a chance to compete in three meets, trying out the new race that I worked hard at every day during Spring Break.

The first meet I competed in, running the hurdles, was at home. I lined up in my starting blocks, waiting to hear, "On your marks, get set, pow!" Once the gun sounded, I got a good takeoff from the blocks. I came to the first hurdle and skimmed over the top. At the next hurdle, I skimmed the top and barely tapped my knee. That is a good sign in this race because you need to be as close to the hurdle as possible. This continued down the track as we were all together in a pack. About halfway down the track, I saw a guy from the corner of my eye. He was two lanes over. I remember him hitting the hurdle, stumbling down the lane, and hitting the hard asphalt. I continued to push through and keep my form. I ended up coming in 2nd place, right behind the 1st place winner. We were neck and neck, and he barely edged me out. I thought to myself, "I found my race, and now it's on."

The last two meets proved to be the same outcome, as I got 1st place in the very next meet and 2nd in the last meet. My coach seemed more excited than I was and told me that next season I was going to be a star for the track team. I didn't know how true that would be, but I was definitely up for the challenge and enjoyed running the hurdles. After I found my race and people began to notice what I was doing in the hurdles, my life changed.

As my junior year in high school was coming to an end, we were all upset that our senior friends were leaving us soon. We made a lot of memories, and I could only think that time was going by fast. I would be in the same position next year, and I still didn't know what I wanted to do. I knew I wanted to play sports in college, preferably football. The only thing was that I wasn't the starting QB during my junior year, and the coaches at my school only seemed to help certain individuals. For some reason, the football coaches would push and get letters from some kids saying they were good friends with their parents. I knew this wasn't right and that I would have to fight my way through the red tape if I even wanted a chance at a scholarship for next year. I couldn't depend on the coaches to help me because I didn't grow up in this town, and I was considered an outcast, a kid that was good at sports but wouldn't make it in life. I had to do what it took to get a scholarship, make my own game film, and contact the colleges I was interested in playing for. I had the mindset that nobody was going to do it for me. I had to fight my whole life for everything I had up to this point, and I wasn't about to stop now. It was the end of the year, but to me, it was going to be the beginning of how the rest of my life would play out.

CHAPTER 13
The Final Year

THIS SUMMER WAS going to prove to be a little different. Due to the misdemeanor underage drinking charges I had received, I appeared in court in Tucson. I received a $200 fine and 80 hours of community service. I knew this wouldn't be as fun a summer as the rest because now I would be working in the scorching summer heat, cutting grass, and painting a fire station. This was part of my 80 hours of community service. I would work my hours daily, and the man at the fire station would log my hours. It took me a couple of weeks to complete my hours, but I finally got them done and was finished with my punishment. Now I could finally be free. It was like trouble was all around me at the end of the year leading into summer, and I needed to get back on track and focus.

Monique went to see her dad in Phoenix for a couple of weeks, and during this time, I was training, lifting weights, and, of course, partying on the weekends. As the two weeks went by very quickly, she came back, and I was excited to see her. She shared with me everything that was going on with her family. She was sad that some things were happening that she had no control over. She also didn't like that her mom and dad were continuously arguing over her being down here instead of with them. I let her know I understood. We were in my house alone and sitting on my bed. We both told each other how much we missed being together. I shared with her my exciting experiences of community service and everything I went through. She thought I was crazy and hit me, telling me that I could have ended up in jail. I agreed, and somehow she ended up closer to me, and we started making out. One thing led to another, and this was the first time of many that we made love to each other. While we were in the middle of making love, we didn't hear the front door open. Monique was going down on me, and my mom opened the blanket and asked what we were doing. She was confused and didn't know how to react. I was confused and embarrassed when my mom walked in on my girlfriend and me. Monique was very embarrassed. We both got dressed and walked into the living room, where my mom sat with an angry look. Monique apologized and proceeded to leave. Once she left, my mom yelled at me, told me that I shouldn't be doing that kind of stuff, and asked what would happen if she ended up pregnant. Everything she said went in one ear and out the other, as I already had my mind about what I would do. I planned on being with Monique forever. Nobody could stop us from being together, and we would do what we wanted. My mom was only mad at me for about one day, and everything returned to normal. The next time I saw Monique was two days later because she wanted to give everything time to cool off, which I understood. It had to be devastating for a female to be caught doing something like that by another female, especially to their son. I could only imagine what was going through her mind.

This was going to be my last and final summer, and I was determined to make the best of it. I saw one of the senior graduates, Adam, at the corner store. He asked me if I wanted to hang out and if I needed a ride. I told him sure. When I got in the car with Adam and four of his friends, they lit up a blunt. They passed it to me, coughing, laughing, and telling me to take a hit. The windows were rolled up, and I did not want to be a punk, so I took a hit of the blunt. We were all laughing and joking until I suddenly started panicking. I couldn't breathe, and the windows were up, which didn't help. I didn't know what was happening and thought I was about to die. This couldn't be a regular weed because I thought weed calms you down. They unlocked the doors, and we all got out. They were all laughing and joking, and I couldn't do anything but cough and spit up on the ground. To this day, I don't know what was in that "weed" and if I was set up, but I have never tried smoking weed again. I have never tried smoking anything, including a cigarette.

I couldn't let my summer start like this. I was determined to stay focused, work to earn money, and train hard for this upcoming sports season. I went with my friend Mike Riesgo and his dad because they had an orange Firebird car they were selling. I was determined to have a car during my senior year. I wasn't going to be a star athlete and not have a car of my own. I would go to their house and mow their lawn every week until I finally got a job at Burger King. I was working all day, and when I wasn't at work, I was training for the upcoming football season. Mike's dad called me to the house and told me that I could get the car with a down payment and that he would let me make small payments every month until it was paid off. Of course, I was ecstatic! I finally got my own car and didn't have to depend on anyone to give me rides anymore. The rest of the summer, I was working at Burger King and trying to earn as much money as possible for gas and, of course, for clothes and gifts for Monique. I had to have lunch money as I would take her out every day for lunch. While working at Burger King, one of the older guys who had already graduated told me I could make even more money if I did what he did. I was curious because, of course, I wanted to make more money. After all, what high school kid didn't, right?

This older guy told me that when I charge someone for their meal, I should always keep a dollar and not give them the correct change back. Also, if I were working the drive-thru, I would overcharge them and keep the extra money they gave me. I thought this was the craziest idea, and nobody would fall for it. I watched him do it a few times, and it worked. By the night's end, he had over $70 in his pocket just from overcharging people. I couldn't believe this worked. I hadn't stolen anything since the day we robbed the lady's house in Tucson. Although I didn't like the feeling, I needed more money, and my checks weren't that great. I started to do as my friend did, and the first night I had about $35. I didn't get caught, and it was very easy. The next time I worked, I worked at the drive-thru and did it again. This time I made over $75. Wow, I couldn't believe how easy this was. People weren't paying attention to how much they were being charged. They weren't even checking how much change they were receiving back from me. I couldn't believe how easy this was. After I got really brave, I was making over $100 a day just from overcharging naive people.

Finally, the first day of school came, and now I was the big senior on campus. This was going to be my year because I worked so hard throughout my last three years and the summer to make it great. I was excited about this year. The roster was posted for the starting positions for our last year of high school football. This time I made the starting QB position! Everything was beginning to fall into place. I had a car, was a senior, and was the starting QB for our varsity football team. It was Friday and our first varsity game, and I had butterflies because this would be my first time starting as QB for the varsity. Everything was going to fall on my shoulders. Our team was ranked #1 in the state. We had the state's #1 and #3 running backs, and I was the player to watch. I can remember in that first game, we absolutely destroyed our opponents. I don't think they even scored against our defense. Our defense was brutal, and I was able to play starting safety as well. At least until I got a concussion. I remember running straight towards this short, thick running back, coming straight up the middle of the line. He broke through the line and past our linebackers. I was running full steam ahead and blasted straight into him. We both went backward, our feet flying into the air. My teammates said I curled up like a cat. They helped me off the field once I came to my senses. Ms. Lamb was our trainer then and told me I couldn't go back into the game. I couldn't take just sitting on the sidelines watching while my team was struggling without me. I put my helmet on and ran back onto the field like I was supposed to be out there. Roo was my running back, and he also had a concussion but was still in the game. We were at the 10-yard line, and I called a play. The only person that understood what I was saying was Roo. I handed the ball off, and Roo broke two tackles to take the ball into the end zone for a score. We were back on top, and nobody stopped us from staying undefeated. Ms. Lamb saw me in the game and was furious. She asked me how I got back out there, and I told her I had to play so we could win. She took me back out of the game, and this would also be the last time I played safety for the rest of the season. The coaches didn't want to risk losing me as their starting QB.

Homecoming week is another memory that I will never forget. We were playing a team called Tombstone. It wasn't even really a game; we were demolishing this team. At half-time, the score was roughly 30-0. Everyone returned to the locker room except the Homecoming King and Queen nominees. I was called a nominee, and I was shocked, as I didn't expect this at all. Evidently, everyone voted for the school's top 5 males and females to be Homecoming King and Queen. All of the nominees lined up on the field. The announcer gave information about each candidate. Then they would begin to announce the 2nd runners-up. It wasn't me, so I didn't think anything of it. I was hoping to hurry up and get off the field to see our game plan for the 3rd quarter. Next, he announced the 1st runners-up. Again, it wasn't me, and I thought this was taking too long. Could we hurry up and get this over with already? Finally, he announced the Homecoming Queen first, and it was Karin Crawford. That was cool, but there were only two guys left, and why did I stand out here looking crazy when I could be in the locker room with my team? Karin walked forward to the sideline, staring at the crowd. Everyone was cheering as they gave her some flowers, strapped the homecoming queen wrap around her body and put the crown on her head. Next, they announced the Homecoming King. The announcer said, "Senior, Jason Mitchell!" I wasn't paying attention and didn't hear my name called. I wasn't expecting my name to be called. I just wanted to get off the field. Everyone cheered. Karin was looking at me, and the other two nominees started clapping. I was puzzled, then realized that my name had just been called. Wow! Is this really happening? I walked forward to the sideline where Karin was standing. They put the Homecoming King's wrap around my body and the crown on my head. All I remember is everyone cheering very loudly. I was still in shock! Karin congratulated me, and I told her congratulations as well. She grabbed my arm, and we got into the vehicle and took a lap around the track, waving at everyone. This was an amazing experience to know that everyone in the school voted for me to be their Homecoming King. I was forever grateful. We eventually went on to win the game 52-0.

We went undefeated that season and blew out every team we played. It was time to head into the playoffs, where the wins counted. This couldn't be like last year when we blew it in the first round. We were expected to win state this year, and that was what we were going to do. We beat all the teams during the playoffs, and I continued to play like Randall Cunningham. He was my favorite player. Like Randall, I would wear one glove on my left hand and dive into the end zone on my head. I was known as Little Randall. I even had the same #12 jersey as Randall. I had to help my team win this championship. We would be playing for the state championship title game against another undefeated school named St. Johns. The thing about St. John's is that they would recruit the best players possible to play for them. We didn't do this. We all became one family and played like a team, which got us to this point. It was the night of the state championship game, and our bus pulled into the school in Phoenix where we would be playing. I hadn't been sacked all year, which was rare for a QB. Some students made a banner that said, "Yet To Be Sacked #12!" They posted this banner on St. John's bus before the game and made sure all their players saw it. It was a nice night, and the temperature in Phoenix was about 65 degrees. It was the first week of December, and for us, this was perfect football weather. We lost the coin toss and went on defense first. We lined up for the kickoff. When the referee blew the whistle, Max kicked the ball with everything he had. The ball sailed to the 15-yard line, where Marcus Bell took the kickoff. He ran the kick return all the way back for the first score of the game. We were confused because nothing like this had ever happened to our team before. The most points ever scored against us in a single game was 12 points. As the game went on, the moment came when I took the snap from my center in the 2nd quarter. I dropped back to pass, and nobody was open. I started to scramble, running back and forth as the defense closed in on me. It seemed like I was scrambling for 5 minutes before they finally sacked me for a 15-yard loss. This was my first sack of the season, and St. John's celebrated like they had just won the championship game. It seemed like our defense couldn't hold Marcus Bell, and our offense couldn't get the ball into the end zone. Time began to wind down, and the score was 36-0 in favor of St. John's. I remember our defense arguing with each other on the field because nobody did anything like this to us the entire season. Finally, we scored a touchdown but missed the extra point. The clock ticked down to zero, and the final score was 36-6. I had over 160 yards passing this game and ran for over 60 yards. For some reason, our offense couldn't get the ball into the end zone. Marcus Bell ran all over us, returned a kickoff and punted for a touchdown, and couldn't be stopped. Once the game was over, we all cried like babies that night in the middle of the field. This was our first loss as a team during our high school years. We were expected to win the state, and once again, we were so close but so far. St. John's wound up being 44-0, as they didn't lose a game in 3 or 4 years. The whole state of Arizona came out to watch this game, and I felt like we let the fans down. I still have memories to this day of this game. It is one of the worst feelings to lose the state championship game when your team is expected to win it all. Marcus Bell went on to play for the University of Arizona and was drafted by the Seattle Seahawks as a linebacker in 2000. He later played for the Detroit Lions as well, before his NFL career was over. It was a great season, although we lost the state championship. We finished 12-1, and once we returned to our hometown, we felt the love and appreciation for the hard work we had put in all year. It was definitely appreciated!

CHAPTER 14

Finish Strong

FOOTBALL SEASON WAS over, and next up was wrestling. I had been waiting for this moment since last year. I was expected to be one of the top wrestlers in the state for my weight class of 145lbs. On the first day of practice, I was ready, in great shape and ready to take on the world. I ran our normal 6-mile route through the sandy wash and came back first. Once everyone returned, we hit the mat and did conditioning drills. I did great during the drills and wasn't nearly as tired as I usually was in the previous three years. My body felt great, I was stronger, my technique and skills were better, and I was much faster this year. After wrestling practice, I got in my car and drove home. It was Friday night, around 9 pm. I was tired once I got home, so I fell straight asleep. The next morning, when I woke up, Joe was yelling and harassing me for no apparent reason. He wanted me to get a shovel and start working in the yard, mixing cement and building the rock wall. I was mad because I had been working hard at practice and at Burger King, and now I couldn't even rest in my own home. This was the first time I cursed in front of my parents, and I told him to f-off. I told him he wasn't my dad and couldn't tell me what to do. By this time, he was already angry and started coming toward me. Joe was 6'6" and weighed about 250lbs. I wasn't trying to stick around for him to get his hands on me. I took off running, and our road had a hill that I had been running for the last three years. I was used to it. Joe was fast for about 5-7 seconds, but once he hit that hill, he gave out of breath and stopped chasing me. I remember him telling me not to come back, and if I did, he would kill me. I kept going until I got to Monique's house. I banged on her door until she came out. She asked me what had happened, and I told her. She told me to give it time and then I could go back home. I told her that I thought I really messed up this time. Joe was very angry, and if I went back, nothing good was going to come out of it. We stayed up all night and talked about what I should do. Going back home wasn't an option. My only other option was to give Gabe a call and see if I could stay over at his place until everything cooled down. Early the next morning, we went to the store, and I used the payphone to call Gabe. I told him what had happened, and he said he would be right over to pick me up. I didn't have any clothes or a toothbrush. I told Gabe to drive close to my house so I could see if my parents were home. The truck wasn't in the yard, so I figured they were gone. We pulled up to my house, and I quickly went inside and got my clothes. I came out with everything I needed and put it in the car. When we were getting ready to leave, my mom and Joe pulled up. I was ready to take off again, but my mom told me that Joe wasn't going to do anything. He promised he wouldn't touch me, and we talked about what had happened the previous night. We eventually came to terms with the fact that I wouldn't be living at home anymore. I was 17 years old, and I was about to be homeless.

Once again, Gabe offered for me to stay at his house. I asked him if he was sure and if his mother, Rosemary, would let me stay there until I finished school. I had a lot going for me in sports this year, and the last thing I needed was to be homeless on the streets with no place to go, dropping out of high school my senior year. When we got to Gabe's house, we told his mom what had happened. She told me it was fine that I could come and stay with them as long as I needed. I was grateful and definitely wouldn't mess this opportunity up. Rosemary took me in like I was her son. She cooked and always asked if I needed anything. Around this time, my car had broken down, and I needed something new to get back and forth to practice and work. I searched in the newspaper and couldn't find anything. Gabe told me we should look in Tucson because they always have good deals on used cars. I agreed, and we got in his car and headed to Tucson. We looked around for about an hour until we found a lemon lot with some cars in it that were fairly priced. There was a white Ford Escort that caught my eye and was priced at $1,200. The car salesman told me I could get the car for $100 down and $100 a month. He couldn't be serious! This was a great deal, so I signed the paperwork and took the car that evening. I was happy I found such a great deal because I wouldn't know what I was going to do for work if I didn't have a car.

I went back to school and continued taking Monique to lunch, and we would talk about the things going on in my life. She always encouraged me and told me that I could graduate and do great in sports. Once I graduated and got a scholarship, I could get out of this city. I would go to wrestling practice. This year it was a breeze. I didn't have anybody in my weight category that could come close to beating me in a challenge. I had the varsity spot on lock, and I was going to be a state champion. Jimmy Rivera and Eli were both in different weight classes this year, so things were looking bright for me. As the season went on, I continued to win match after match. There were a few close matches, but I came out on top. The only time I lost during the season was during our home invitational. I was about 8lbs over my weight, and the teachers let me out of class to run in the gym during the entire day. I wore a sweat suit under my regular sweats and ran laps around the gym for about 2-3 hours. I lost weight, but I was out of energy, especially because I didn't eat anything all day. When the weigh-ins arrived, I was half a pound underweight. I was starving. Once the weigh-in was over, I stuffed my face with bananas and cheeseburgers.

The first match was devastating. I didn't have any energy, and my opponent was basically doing anything he wanted to me. I couldn't use my strength, speed, or skills, as I couldn't even function properly. I ended up losing that match and dropping to the consolation bracket. Now there was no way to get into 1st place. The best chance I had was to go for 3rd place. I was feeling tired and weak and knew it wouldn't be a good night for me. My second match wasn't much better. In the same way the first match turned out, so did the second match. Again, I lost by points, and this time, I was eliminated from the tournament. I was expected to win the invitational. I was one of the best wrestlers in the state in my weight class, and now I was eliminated in my hometown! I watched the rest of the tournament from the bleachers as I was very angry for letting myself get that much overweight. As the rest of the year went on, I continued to stay within 1-2 pounds of my wrestling weight. I dominated my weight class, and once the state championships came, I was even more ready than I was at the beginning of the year. I knew all of my competitors, and I could beat every last one of them. I was flying through the state championship tournament until I got to one opponent I had never faced before. We were going back and forth the entire match. In the 3rd period, with about 5 seconds left, I was down by 2 points. I was on the bottom and had 5 seconds left to escape and score a takedown to move on to the final match for the state championship. The referee blew the whistle, and I exploded to my feet, escaped from his grasp, and immediately took him down to the mat. The referee claimed the time had expired by the time I took him down. My coach argued that there was 1 second left when he hit the mat. The referee didn't budge and gave the win to my opponent. I was furious because I knew I should be going to the final match for 1st place! Now I would be wrestling for 3rd or 4th place. I pinned my opponent during the final match and took 3rd place at the state championships. The guy that slipped by me ended up winning the state championship, and I was so angry because I knew that should be me standing up there. Our team did an outstanding job overall, and we represented our school very well. My coach told me he was proud of me and that I had come a long way. He ensured that I didn't get disappointed with the outcome of the finals and knew that I gave it my best. I understood, but it seemed like this was beginning to be a drought my senior year. We lost the state championship in football, and now I lost the state championship in wrestling. I didn't want to settle for 3rd place.

When I got home, Gabe's mom congratulated me and told me to keep my head up. She said I did very well and that she had watched me progress through my high school years. I nodded and agreed with her. I told her thank you and that I would continue to work hard. Monique told me she was proud of how far I had come. She told me not to take any of this for granite, especially after everything that I had been through this year.

All of the frustration from everything I was facing was starting to bottle up inside me. One weekend, Gabe and I were riding to the store when we saw one of these wanna-be gang bangers with his girlfriend and Nathan Tamez. We already didn't get along too well at school. We would always talk crap to each other, but nothing ever came of it. On this particular night, around midnight, Nathan got brave and told me to meet him by the park so we could fight. After we exchanged some heated words, we got in the car, and they followed us to the park. Once there, we parked, and I got out, and Nathan was standing in the parking lot. Gabe got out and told the wanna-be gang banger and his girlfriend not to interfere because this was between Nathan and me. Once we walked toward each other, Nathan threw the first punch and missed. I ducked and came back with a hard right hand, which connected straight to his eye, and he fell backward. I moved toward him and kicked him in the ribs. I glanced up, and his friend had a long sword in his hand. He started coming towards me. I began backing up, and when he came at me in a full sprint, I took off in a full sprint as well. He ran behind me for about half a mile until I came up on some people's porch and banged on the door for them to let me in. This guy was trying to kill me and would have stabbed me with this sword if he had caught me. Once the people opened the door, he turned around and ran back to his car. They took off, and the cops came about 10 minutes later to where we were in the park. They asked me what had happened, and I told them that we were being jumped by some people I'd never seen before. I wasn't a snitch, so the last thing I was going to do was tell on these dudes. The cop didn't believe me, but he let Gabe and me go. He told us to stay out of trouble and be careful. We left and laughed about the situation the whole way back to Gabe's house.

Later that evening, I went out with Monique, and we were drinking. We got into an argument, and after we were done with each other, I dropped her off, got in my car, and left. I returned to Gabe's house as drunk as I had ever been. I knocked on his window because I didn't want his mom to know I was drunk and coming home late. Gabe told me to go to the door, and he let me in. Rolando and Eric were also staying over at Gabe's that night. I remember going to sleep on the bed. All of us were in the same room. Eric and Rolando were on the floor. Gabe was in the living room. They told me that I got up in the pitch dark and stepped on Rolando while trying to get to the door. I couldn't see anything, and I started tearing up the whole room, trying to get out. Meanwhile, Jenny Meza was trying to sneak in to see Lindsay. She saw me through the window, freaked out, and started screaming, running down the street. I fell back onto the bed and went right back to sleep. Gabe and his mom both opened the door and turned on the light. I was asleep. Eric and Rolando were both sitting up, trying to figure out what had just happened. Rosemary thought Rolando and Eric were fighting. They both told Rosemary that I had started tearing up the room and didn't know what was happening. Rosemary didn't believe them at first because I was sound asleep. The next morning, Rosemary asked if I remembered what had happened last night, and I didn't have a clue. They told me the details, and we couldn't do anything but laugh. From then on, Rolando and Eric didn't want to stay in the same room with me at night. We would always joke about that night and what happened.

Track season was now about to begin. Once again, I was expected to do extremely well and possibly take state in the 110M and 300M intermediate hurdles. I was determined and bound to finish the school year with some kind of championship before graduating. Everything else seemed to fall short, and this was my last chance. After school, we would practice, and I felt very good about the upcoming season after every practice. My form was excellent, and my speed was improving. We would begin our track meets, and I would blow out the competition by over 5-6 seconds. There was nobody that was coming close to beating me as the season went on.

During one particular track meet, we went out of town for an invitational. The boys and girls all rode on the same bus. I remember Monique and I were fighting at the time, and we hadn't spoken to each other in over four days. There was a girl that always flirted with me during the entire season and made it known that she really liked me. I would always tell her that I had a girlfriend, but this didn't stop her, especially during this trip. On the way to the meet, we ended up sitting together, and she would put her hand on my private parts and ask me if I wanted her. I would continue telling her I had a girlfriend, and this wasn't right. She still didn't care. She would kiss me on my neck and rub my leg. Although I didn't want to at the time, I finally gave in, and we ended up kissing. While we were at the invitational meet, all I could think about was our kiss on the way to the track meet. I warmed up for my event, and once it was time for my race, I won with no competition at the time. I put my track jumpsuit back on and went to the bus to take a nap before my next race later that day. This girl was on the bus. She smiled at me and told me to come back to where she was, which was about ¾ towards the back of the bus. As stupid as I was, I did and sat in the same seat as her. We ducked down into the seat and started kissing and making out. The next thing I knew, my shorts were down, and she was sitting on top of me. Before I knew it, we were having sex on the school bus at the track meet with the bus driver sitting at the front of the bus. He didn't pay us any attention, at least I don't think he did because he didn't say anything. About 15 minutes later, we were both putting our shorts back on, and it was time for me to go back to the track to get ready for my 300 intermediate hurdles race. The whole time, this moment with her was flashing through my mind. Once the race started, I took off as fast as I usually did. I started to slow down around the last 100 meters and was passed by another guy who was my only competition in this race. I ended up in 2nd place at this invitational in the 300 intermediate hurdles. I was furious and couldn't believe what had happened.

The bus ride home that evening was interesting as we sat together, made out some more, and vowed never to let anyone know what happened. Every time I saw this girl in school or at a party the rest of the year, she would smirk and smile. I would fall for her a few times and even go to her house while her parents were gone just to have more sex. She was shaped very nicely and had a big butt, which I loved. At this point, I was careless and didn't care much anymore.

I would go on to win the rest of my races in the 110 meter hurdles and the 300 intermediate hurdles. I was heading to the Arizona State Championships. Everything from the beginning of the year until now just kept playing through my head. I didn't want this to be another mishap like my football and wrestling seasons. Everything was going smoothly, and now it was time for the top 8 positions to take the starting blocks. The 110 meter hurdle finals were about to begin. There were two other guys that were really good and my only competition. It was going to be a great race. As we lined up on the starting blocks, butterflies raced through my stomach, and I was as nervous as I could be. Once we took our positions, I could hear the man give the commands. His arm went up in the air with the gun pointed to the sky. Runners on your marks! Get set! Pow! We all took off. We hit the first hurdle, second hurdle, and third hurdle. The other two competitors and I were neck and neck. As we got close to the end, my knee dropped lower than it should have and hit the last hurdle. I beat all of these guys during the regular track season. Now, one of the guys goes ahead of me by about a head. We sprint to the finish line, and once again, it happens. I got 2nd place! I beat this guy all season, and just because of one minor mistake, I am now back in 2nd place. This couldn't be happening. There were college scouts in the crowd, and they were all watching us. My coach told me to run the best race I could because he knew a scout from Pima College was there specifically to watch me race. This was terrible! How could I let this happen? The same thing would happen later that evening once we began the 300 intermediate hurdle race. I wasn't running as hard as I should have and miscalculated, which cost me the first place position. I ended up taking 2nd place in this race as well. It was like I couldn't get a first place victory to save my life during my last year. I was expected and predicted to, but I just couldn't pull it off. Even to this day, I still claim both the wrestling and track state championships because I beat both of those guys all year. I couldn't face the fact that I didn't take home the championships when, in reality, they should be mine.

CHAPTER 15

The Last Summer

THE SPORTS SEASON was coming to a close, and the school year was nearing its end. It was a great year. There were some disappointments, but for the most part, I did extremely well in all three sports. Everyone was proud of me due to the circumstances that I was in and overcame, and now I am graduating. What would lie ahead for my future? Letters started coming in from different schools for sports scholarships. I wanted to play football, and a letter from Central Iowa came in. They wanted me to come to play football for them as a wide receiver. My mentality at the time was that there were no black people in Iowa, and I wasn't about to go there to be lynched. All of the other scholarships that looked good were for track. I signed up with Pima Community College's track and wrestling team for a full-ride scholarship. All of my books and tuition would be paid for! This was awesome. I was one of the kids the teachers thought wouldn't succeed due to my circumstances, yet I proved them wrong again.

School ended, and the summer was upon us. It would be our last time partying with all of the high school kids we knew over the years before we headed off to college. We would party every weekend, and Monique and I would get into small fights.

We would fight about me going to college and how everything was going to work. She knew I was an athlete; even in school, I would have other girls do my homework to ensure I passed and stayed eligible. Now I am going to college in the fall. I would be around more mature, older college girls with college parties every night. She wasn't too excited, but I knew I wanted to be with her for life. We would continue attending parties, and one particular party on July 4th was out in the desert area that we rarely went to. Something didn't seem quite right on this night. I pulled up, and there were a lot of cars parked there, so I knew the party was jumpin. Everyone was drinking, laughing, and having a good time. There was this kid at our school named Chris, who I was friends with. Chris was a good kid but tried to be involved with gangs in Tucson. Many of his cousins were from Tucson, and he was always up there. I was pretty good friends with Chris and didn't know he had a beef with this new kid who moved to our school from Tucson. Apparently, he got kicked out of school in Tucson, and they made him transfer to our school. This kid was heavily involved in gangs, went to a juvenile detention center a few times, and was expelled from the school he regularly attended due to being involved in gangs. At this party, Chris and this kid were getting into it, but the fight was broken up before it started. I remember standing next to Chris while talking to someone else. Out of nowhere, this kid comes back with a knife and stabs Chris in the chest. I saw Chris falling to the ground and blood running down his white T-shirt. The kid took off running, hopped into a car, and sped off with some of his friends. Chris was lying there and starting to fade away. We were trying to keep him awake, but by the time the ambulance and police arrived, Chris had died. Everyone was devastated and couldn't believe what had just happened. This guy always made us laugh, but unfortunately, his life was taken in an instant. The cops caught the kid that stabbed Chris and took him in. A couple of months later, he went to trial and was acquitted. They said he stabbed Chris in self-defense and was let off the hook. I can remember so many people being furious about what had happened. Now, this guy was being let off the hook for killing someone. This couldn't be happening! After this devastating outcome, parties were still happening during the summer, but we never forgot what happened to Chris. It seemed like the entire city came out for Chris's funeral to pay their respects. He was only a young junior in high school with a long life ahead of him until it was taken.

During the summer, I continued to work at Burger King and make some extra money by ripping people off. Finally, one day, Ms. Oma caught me and asked me what I was doing. I told her I had mistakenly counted wrong, but she didn't fall for it. She told me that I was a really good kid and I didn't need to get caught up in something like theft or robbery, which I was doing. I told her that I agreed and wouldn't let it happen again. My hours started getting cut short, and after a while, it wasn't even worth me working there any longer.

Summer was coming to an end, and my new world was about to begin. Monique and I decided to stay together. However, she was moving back to Phoenix since I was leaving for college. During this time, I was sad, but at the same time, I knew college would be fun and, hopefully, my mind would be occupied enough to keep it off of her. Since I didn't have to pay for any classes or books, all I had to do was show up for school on the first day and go to class.

It was bitter-sweet as we all had one last party and said our goodbyes to each other. Some people were putting off college until the next year, and some of us were leaving right as the summer was over. We definitely had some great memories and would definitely miss each other. Whether we fought or laughed, it seemed like we all grew up together as one big happy family. We all depended on each other and helped each other when we were down. We shared many memories and laughs along the way, and it was amazing to watch so many of us grow into the people we had become. There were a couple of people with football scholarships that were headed both out of state and to the Phoenix area. Some of the guys had wrestling scholarships to Arizona State University and a few other places. Others had baseball scholarships. Few of us had track scholarships. All in all, this would be our last and final time together.

We partied like this was the last party we would attend. Everyone had a great time as we played all of our favorite music and drank until we couldn't drink anymore. We talked about the good and bad times. We reminisced about everything we had been through, and, of course, I had to bring back some of my raps for everyone. We discussed our hopes and dreams, and everyone exchanged information. We all vowed to keep in touch. After the night ended and the brink of sunrise was beginning to rise, we all hugged, got in our cars and one by one left. I remember being one of the last ones to leave with Monique. We stared at everyone leaving. I have never felt like this before. I was actually about to be a grown man. Although I was going to be a grown man, a tear fell from my eye because I didn't want this to end deeply. It was all I knew, and my teammates had become my new family. Once again, everything was being torn and ripped away from me. My girlfriend was returning to Phoenix, my friends were going to different colleges, and I felt like I had nothing left. What if I don't succeed? What if I turned out to be a failure like my teachers from throughout the years claimed I would be? So many thoughts ran through my mind, and I felt like I wasn't ready for what was about to come next in my life.

The day arrived when Monique was leaving to head back to Phoenix. Would we ever see each other again? How would this long-distance relationship thing work? Would I find someone else in college? Would she find someone in her high school class? So many thoughts and insecurities came across both of our minds that we could only deal with them the best way we knew how. We continued to have fun, laugh, and share all the memories we had made over the last couple of years. As the night was ending and the morning was starting to come with quickness, we were intimate with each other for what may have been the last time. She lay on my chest, and I held her close as I was losing my best friend, and there was no telling what might happen to us once she left to head home. As the morning came, I helped her pack and gather her stuff. We hugged one last time, and she started crying. She didn't want to leave, and I didn't want her to leave. Eventually, she got in the car with her mom, and I could feel my heart drop as I remember seeing her stare at me through the window as the car started to pull off. All I could do was stand there, wave, and try to be as strong as I could for her. This was it. Everything was moving way too fast.

CHAPTER 16
It All Begins

SUMMER ENDED, AND I was bound to find a job or two in Tucson because I needed party money for college. I couldn't be a star athlete and not have any funds to have fun. I was still staying at Gabe's house, and I would have to drive back and forth about 40 miles each way to go to work and school. I got hired as a bellboy at Embassy Suites, and within a week, I was hired as a telemarketer for a radio station too. This was bound to give me some money while I was in school.

The first day of college came, and I went to the campus at Pima Community College. I was lost and had no clue where to go. So, like any other hungry kid would do, I went straight to the cafeteria. It was a large facility and seemed to be the hangout spot for many students. There were big round tables where all the students gathered around and talked while they waited for their next class to begin. I sat at one of the empty round tables and opened my Gatorade that I already had with me. I began to take a drink, and then I heard this soft voice behind me with a tap on the shoulder asking if she could sit down. When I turned around and looked, there was this beautiful, nicely shaped Hispanic girl. Of course, I said yes! She was very attractive and had mesmerizing eyes that were very easy to get lost in.

She told me her name was Veronica, and I told her mine was Jason. We talked for about an hour until I had to go to my first class. We exchanged numbers, and she told me that she hoped she would get to see me again. I could tell that this girl was very flirty. She told me she was from a city called Nogales. Nogales was approximately one and a half hours away from Tucson. She would drive to school from her city and stay there all day until her classes were over.

I walked into my first class, and it had about 25 students. Everyone seemed so focused and ready to learn. The teacher walked into the class, introduced himself, and immediately began writing math problems on the board. I was not used to this. Typically, the first few days of school are spent getting to know one another and becoming acquainted with the books. He was already talking about 50 math questions for homework, and this was only our first day. The next class was English. I walked to my class, and it was the same scenario as in the math class. All the students were in there, sitting so properly, pens and pencils in hand, with a sheet of paper ready for note-taking. These were some serious nerds! Why wasn't anyone clowning and telling jokes? Everyone was actually paying attention and eager to learn. I didn't know anything about this college stuff. After what I saw, I thought this might not be the life for me. I continued to attend each class with the same outcome. I felt so lost as a freshman. It almost reminded me of my freshman year in high school. Finally, classes were over, and it was time for my first track practice. We got dressed and went to the track, where we would meet with the rest of the track team and work on off-season practice drills. After we all introduced ourselves, the coach handed us a sheet of paper with our exercises, sets, and reps. The first running exercise we had was to run these steep hills that were behind the gym. It was a paved street road with a huge steep hill. Some of the guys that were on the team from last year seemed to roll through the drills like it was nothing. This was the first time in a long time that I was actually struggling and breathing hard during practice. Man, this was tough! I couldn't believe I was this out of shape. By the end of practice, I was so glad it was over. The only thing was that I still had to go to my telemarketing job on that same day and drive 45 minutes home. I definitely wasn't looking forward to that.

On the first day, I pulled up to my telemarketing job and walked into the building. I received a script from the manager and proceeded to my assigned table so I could sit down. I was sitting at a desk with a tape recorder-like machine and walls on either side. I had a stack of papers to write all the reports from the calls I made and a never-ending list of phone numbers. The room was cloudy and filled with cigarette smoke from the smokers. This facility did not have a no-smoking policy. The only thing that kept me going at this place was the girl that sat next to me. Her name was Amy, and she was from Phoenix. She was also attending Pima Community College. She was more on the serious side, but I made her laugh by distracting her from her phone calls. We got along well and talked for quite some time every time we went on break. Amy told me that she had an apartment in Tucson in a nice location. She had a boyfriend in Phoenix, but he didn't want to move down to Tucson. She needed someone to move in as a roommate and help her with some of her bills because her dad was going to stop paying for everything the next month. I told her I lived 45 minutes away and needed to be closer to my two jobs, school, and sports. We talked about it a few times, and after she carefully considered my moving in, she finally gave me the green light. Amy was like my sister; we got along well but had our disagreements. She was always used to getting everything her way because her dad spoiled her. I thought about moving in and if it would really work. I weighed all my options, which seemed to be the best choice. Later that evening, I went home and discussed everything with Rosemary and Gabe. Rosemary wanted me to ensure this was what I wanted to do. She was being a protective mom and making sure I wasn't going to get stuck in something unnecessary. I told her that this would be a good move for me and that Amy seemed to be a really cool person. Plus, we hit it off as good friends, and now I consider her like my sister. The next day, I packed all my stuff and put it in my Ford Escort. I headed to Tucson and met Amy at the apartments. They were nice and on the good side of town. They seemed to be newer model apartments and even had a pool that I could see from our balcony. The only issue was that this was a one-bedroom apartment. I didn't plan on being stuck with a girl, and I was still seeing Monique, so messing with Amy was out of the question. She was also pretty crazy, and I often had to calm her down regarding her boyfriend in Phoenix.

Amy told me that there were two beds in the bedroom, and I could sleep on the other bed. She made sure to let me know that nothing was going to happen between us, which I was perfectly fine with. The first night I moved in, we stayed up talking, and she cooked a dish I cannot recall. I just knew it wasn't Ramen Noodles, so I was happy to eat it. I thought that Amy was really cool and that this might work out well. I got into my bed and left the light on because Amy was in the bathroom taking a shower and changing. Once she came out, she wore a small T-shirt and very short shorts. I could almost see all of her goodies. I almost started sweating and had to turn in the opposite direction towards the wall so I wouldn't see her. Amy wasn't a bad-looking girl at all, and she knew it. Every guy at the telemarketing job tried to hit on her, and she shut them all down because she was loyal to her boyfriend, Marcus. She said goodnight and made a little joke that made us laugh. I told her goodnight as well, and we both went to sleep. The next morning, I woke up. I couldn't believe I was in my own apartment and living on my own now. All I could do was smile and be nervous at the same time. I took a shower, got dressed, gathered my books, and put them in my bookbag. I told Amy to have a good day and headed out the door to my car. I drove to school and went straight to the cafeteria, hoping I would see Veronica. I hadn't seen her for about a week, and I was starting to wonder if she had dropped her classes. Once I walked in, I saw her sitting at a table talking to a guy. I didn't think anything of it, so I got my sandwich and drink and sat at another table, making sure she could see me. Once Veronica saw me, she immediately got up in the middle of a conversation with the guy and walked over to my table. She sat down and told me she hadn't seen me in a while. I agreed and told her likewise. We talked for about 30 minutes, and she asked me if I wanted to sit in her car because it was getting crowded in the cafeteria. I agreed, and we went to her car. We sat in the car for about 10 minutes before she asked me if I wanted to kiss her. This girl was gorgeous, and I was a horny college boy, so I told her yes. We proceeded to kiss and make out in the car for about 15 minutes before I had to head to class. I told her to call me that evening and maybe we could get together. Nothing good was on my mind at the time. She told me she would try but couldn't make any promises because she still had to drive back to Nogales. I couldn't offer to have her stay at the apartment because I had a roommate, and my roommate happened to be a female, which made it worse. Amy wouldn't go for a hoochie girl staying at the crib.

I went to class and met Ricky, who seemed like a cool guy. He was into basketball, and Ricky knew where all the best parties were going down. He told me to call him later, and we would connect and hit up a party after I got off work. I told him that sounded like a great idea because it was Friday and I was trying to figure out what I would do for the weekend. After class, I went to work at the Embassy Suites. My shift was from 5-10 pm. This was probably one of the most boring jobs I have ever had. I would help people with their luggage and pick up guests from the airport. Half of the time, I would either go in the storage room, van, or hotel room and nap for an hour or two. After all, I had a radio, and the front desk knew how to get a hold of me. While in the storage room, I received a call that I needed to go to the airport and pick up some guests that had just arrived. I gathered all of the information and headed to the airport. Once I parked, I saw a white scruffy-looking guy coming towards the van with a guitar case, ripped jeans, and scraggly hair. He told me to hold on because four more people were coming. Once they all came out and I helped them get their gear into the van, I knew they had to be important. As we drove down the street, headed back to the hotel, they asked me if I knew who they were. I told them that I didn't have a clue. One guy said that his name was Slash from Guns N' Roses. Once I looked closer at him, I could tell this was Slash because I saw the videos on MTV almost every day. The other guys were from a rock group called "The Sex Pistols." They were famous, but I didn't know much about them. I did know about Slash, though. The conversation back to the hotel was fascinating as all they talked about was getting women, pissing, and defecating on them. I was disgusted as they laughed and asked if I had ever done that to a girl. I told them no and never planned on it. I couldn't wait to get these idiots out of my van so I could have some peace and quiet. I needed to take my nap because tonight, it was going down with my new homie, Ricky.

CHAPTER 17

Caught Up

10:00 PM CAME, and my shift was over. I hurried up, got to my apartment, took a shower, changed, and called Ricky. He told me to pick him up at 11:30 pm and then we would head to this party. Once 11:15 pm came, I headed over to Ricky's apartment. He came out smiling with a bag in his hand. He opened it up and told me to grab one. There was some Corona, Budweiser, and Boons Farm in his bag. His bag was filled with nothing but alcohol. I took a Corona, and we sat in the parking lot while we drank our beer. Once we were done, we headed out, and I was ready to get to the party. We were leaving the good side of town and heading in a direction I was all too familiar with. Southside Tucson. Nothing good ever happened on this side of town, and now I was headed over there to a party.

We pulled up to a house with a bunch of cars in the driveway and parked down the street. We heard music blaring from the house and saw a lot of people on the inside through the window. There were a lot of girls at this party. Once we knocked, a guy with a blue bandana on his head opened the door. I thought to myself, "Here we go again." He welcomed us in and gave us a dap. There was more alcohol in the kitchen than I had ever seen at a party. We opened the sliding glass door and went outside;

three kegs of beer were out there. About fifteen people outside huddled around the kegs, smoking, drinking, laughing, and talking. We decided to hang out back there because it wasn't as crowded. I never liked being in crowded areas.

While we were drinking and talking to some other dudes we had just met, three guys got brave and started moving a keg by the brick wall. One guy hopped up on the brick wall, and the other two grabbed the keg. They picked it up and handed it to the guy on the wall. We were all laughing and asking them fools what they were doing. An older guy opened the glass door and got extremely mad. He yelled at them about trying to steal the keg and told them he would be right back. The guy on the wall dropped the keg over it once they got the keg up to him. Two minutes later, this older guy that was yelling at them earlier came back out with a gun and started shooting randomly. The two guys ran and jumped over the wall, and the guy on top jumped down. They all ran off, but this guy was furious and fired at least six shots. Everyone in the backyard scattered, and the gunman stood at the glass door. We couldn't run back into the house to get away, so all we could do was duck down as far away from him as possible. He popped off a couple more shots before he started yelling at the guys running from the house. He was done shooting and calmly walked back into the house. We all looked at each other, got up, and jumped over the wall. We didn't know if he was going to come back and randomly start shooting again. We sobered up quickly as we ran to the front of the house and jumped into the car. Ricky got in the passenger side, and I pulled off very quickly as he was beginning to close the door. Once we got a couple of blocks away, we heard sirens heading in the direction that we just came from. We looked at each other, laughed, and said we got out right on time. We were underage, and again, I could have easily gotten caught and possibly gone to jail and served more community service time.

I returned to the house and told Amy what had happened, and she told me I was crazy. She hit me and said, "Don't be doing that dumb stuff, boy. You need to stay out of trouble and worry about school and sports." Amy was right, but I wasn't thinking about that at the time. I just wanted to party and, of course, have some fun. The next day, when I woke up, I went to Whataburger, which was right around the corner from my apartment. At the register, I saw a Spanish, curvy, wavy-haired, light-brown-skinned girl. When I walked up to order, she asked me if I went to Pima. I told her yes. I proceeded to order, and once I got done, she took out a pen and ripped apart a piece of paper. She wrote her name, Desiree, and phone number on the paper. She smiled and handed it to me. She told me she got off at 6 pm and was free that night. I took her number and put it in my pocket. I got my food to go, and as she smiled and waved, I waved back and walked out the door. Later that night, I almost forgot that I had Desiree's number. I couldn't find anything going on as it was Sunday. I guess the college kids were getting ready for school on Monday. I asked Amy if she would mind if I brought someone over, and after she drilled me, she finally told me, "no." I called Desiree and invited her over to the apartment. My intention was not to watch a movie. After she came over, she met Amy, and we sat on the couch and talked. Amy said she was going out and would be back later that night. Desiree continued to ask me about Amy and what was up between us. I told her that Amy was like my sister and we were just roommates. She had nothing to worry about. After she finally got over me living with another female, she became comfortable. We ended up going to the bedroom. Once again, I was having sex with a woman I had barely met. After we were done, we went back to the living room, and I told Desiree I had to get up early for school. This was my way of hoping she would leave. After she finally got the hint, she left and told me to call her soon.

Monday came, and it was time to go back to class. After partying and having some interesting encounters during the weekend, homework was the last thing on my mind. I didn't do any of my assignments. The teachers took up all of the homework and assigned us more assignments. This was getting ridiculous. Didn't they know we were in college and needed more free time? We had to work, and there wasn't time for homework. I went to track practice and hit the weight room. To my surprise, Veronica was lifting weights in the weight room in skimpy shorts and a half-shirt. When she saw me, she came over, and we started talking. I told her that I had to lift before I got in trouble with the coach, and afterward, we were also starting wrestling practice. After practice, I walked to my car, and Veronica was parked next to me. I thought she had already left, but she said she wanted to wait for me to finish because we hadn't talked in about a week. She got into my car, and we had a casual conversation. I told her I never see her, so I didn't know what to expect from us. She grabbed my right hand and turned it over. Then she pushed my hand away and said, "No, I can't do it." I was confused and asked what she was talking about. She said that she could read palms but that almost every time she did, something bad happened, or people would get mad at her. I was curious and felt like being entertained at the time, so I asked her how she did it. She showed me a line inside my palm and said that that line represented my lifeline. Of course, I didn't believe her and started joking with her. After I finally got her to give in, I told her to read my palm and let me know the future.

She wouldn't tell me how I was going to pass away. However, she told me that I was going to have twin girls. Again, I laughed and messed with her about her palm reading. I told her I wasn't having any kids. After talking about all of this nonsense, it was beginning to get late. She kissed me and told me that she would see me later. After she got out of the car, I headed home.

I walked into my apartment, and another girl was sitting on the couch. I had never seen her before. Amy came from the back bedroom and introduced us. She told me that her name was Michelle. Michelle was going to be our new roommate. I was now confused because I was about to live with two beautiful girls who both had boyfriends. I wondered how this was going to go over. Michelle was a slender white girl with blonde hair, brown eyes, dimples, and a black girl's butt. This was going to be rough. That weekend, a couple of my old high school friends came to the apartment. Max Schug, Anthony Cobb, Joe Wood, and a few others came through. By this time, I was already over living with two beautiful girls who walked around half-naked when I was there by myself. When my friends came over, they would smile ear to ear and always try to get me to hook them up with one of them. It never worked. A few times, it almost worked, but it never did. We decided to have a party at our apartment that night, which was Friday. Everyone was showing up, we had a lot of beer, and best of all, we had the jacuzzi and swimming pool right in front of our apartment. I remember getting so wasted that I was standing on the edge of the balcony that was on the 2nd floor and telling everyone to watch how I could fly like Superman. As a dumb, athletic college idiot, I jumped off the balcony, and Max was on the sidewalk where I was going to land. He looked up and tried to catch me, but broke my fall enough, so I didn't get hurt. Everyone cheered, and we kept the party going.

I met another girl named Dana later this evening. Dana was African American, light brown skinned, athletic built, with green eyes, and very cute. We talked for most of the night, and she was serious about track. Dana was training to go to the Junior Olympics and was one of the fastest girls in the nation. I didn't believe her at first, but when she changed and put on a bathing suit so she could get in the pool, she had me convinced. She was wearing jeans at the time, so I saw that she had well-built legs, but when I saw them in her swimming suit, her legs were very built and toned like the Olympic track athletes you see on TV. After we sat in the jacuzzi and everyone was leaving, we decided to stay there a little longer. Dana got close to me and straddled me. We began to make out, and the next thing I knew, we were having sex in the jacuzzi. When we were done, we went upstairs to the bedroom and continued because Amy and Michelle went to IHOP to get something to eat. Again, I couldn't believe I just did this, and this time it was unprotected. I wasn't looking for a woman, but it was like it had just happened. After Dana got dressed and left, Amy and Michelle came back and were very loud because they were still tipsy. I told them what had happened, and they called me a "dog." They told me all I wanted was some hoochie girls. We were laughing and teasing each other, and Amy said her neck and back were sore. She asked if I would massage it. I thought the girl was crazy and we couldn't live together if we ended up doing something. I couldn't turn down massaging her because I didn't want to hear her whine, so while Michelle was sitting at the table, I was trying to massage the kinks out of Amy's neck. Thank goodness that was all that happened, and we went to sleep later that evening.

Between school and work, I was beginning to get stressed out and didn't know how I was going to pass my classes and stay eligible for track and wrestling. I was on a full-ride scholarship, and all I had to do was pass my classes. Instead, I never did my work and continued to go to parties, drink, and hook up with girls. On Saturday, Max, I, and about four other guys met at some other party. We went to watch this high school basketball tournament. This was where this kid who was supposed to be the next rising basketball star out of high school was going to be playing. This kid had news reporters around him like he was in the NBA and was killing the other team by himself. This guy played for Shadow Mountain and was known as Mike Bibby. Shadow Mountain put in work that day, and we wanted to see what was up for the night. A few guys at the game invited us to a major party that was taking place that evening. We were invited to the University of Arizona star player Joseph Blair's (former Seattle Supersonics) house for a huge party. The University of Arizona was good this year and went 26-7. We were excited because we knew there would be some girls and a lot of alcohol at the party. When we arrived, the DJ was spinning the music, girls were everywhere, and a lot of the U of A players were there. Some of the players were Ben Davis (former Phoenix Suns), Miles Simon (former Orlando Magic), and Jason Terry (former Milwaukee Bucks). I remember we were only at this party for about 1-½ hours, and people were leaving, heading out to another party. It was around 12 pm, and I didn't feel like going out anymore, so I was going to call one of the girls I had met earlier in the week at the mall. She answered, and I asked if she wanted to come to the apartment and hang out. She said, "yes," and she hoped I would call. I told Max and the other guys I wasn't going, so they all got in Mike's car and left. I left but needed to stop and get gas. About 5 miles down the road, I pulled over to a 7-11 close to where I used to come to see my old friends, Kenji, Djomo, Laquita, and Sister. As I was pumping gas, I noticed a brown El Camino coming down the road with music bumping loud. I didn't pay much attention until they got up close, turned off their headlights, and a guy with a red bandana over his face leaned out the back window and started firing shots. I heard two to three shots hit a tall beam pole about ten feet away from me. It only lasted about five seconds before the car sped off down the street. During this time in Tucson, gangs would randomly do drive-by shootings to initiate new members. I can almost guarantee that I almost lost my life to a gang initiation.

CHAPTER 18
Addicted

AFTER I ALMOST got shot again, I went inside and paid for my gas. I had to hurry up because this girl, Dominique, was waiting for me. I got back in my car and got out of there quickly. I didn't know if these guys were going to come back around and try to finish the job or not. Once I hit the road and got away from the store, I knew I was alright. I turned my music up and rode out. As I got closer to the apartment, I told Dominique I was almost there so she could meet me in the parking lot. She was already on the way. I pulled into the parking lot and saw her parked. I pulled up next to her, and we smiled as we got out of the car. Dominique was an African American with a medium brown complexion, a thick build, and a beautiful smile. She was a nice girl, two years older than me and very mature. Amy was in Phoenix with Marcus for the weekend, and Michelle was with her boyfriend, as she usually was for the night. This meant that I had the entire apartment to myself. I invited Dominique up, and we had some drinks as we talked for a little while. Once again, one thing led to another, and she was in my bed. We randomly saw each other at parties, but it was like we were cool and friends but had our little secret. Whenever we wanted some, we would call each other and then go about our business. Dominique knew I had other girls I was messing with, but she was cool about it. She hooked me up with one of her friends named Melissa. Melissa was crazy. She was medium-built Hispanic and had light-tanned skin, brown eyes, and long brown hair. Melissa told me that every time I made her orgasm, she would buy me clothes. I wasn't going to deny her, although I wasn't as attracted to her as I was to the other females I had messed with.

Now I had all of these girls I was messing with at the same time for various reasons and on different occasions. I had one that would buy me clothes for sex; one that worked at a fast food restaurant and would give me free food; one that I was cool with and could get it anytime I wanted; one I would go out with on occasion; and last but not least, a future Olympic track star. I was trying to balance all of this with work and school, and I was still supposedly dating Monique. Monique came over to the apartment about two times the entire time I lived there. We kept in contact, but it started to fade now that I was a male whore and wanted to party all the time. There were even a few times when I saw Cecilia and Laura at a couple of parties and almost ended up hooking up with Cecilia again. Somehow it never happened, and the timing wasn't right, which may have been a good thing. Seeing her at these parties, mixed with the alcohol in my system, triggered my old feelings for her.

One day, there was a knock on the door while I was sitting in my apartment watching TV. It was Dana, and she looked worried, with tears in her eyes. I told her to come in and asked her what was wrong. Amy was in the kitchen cooking at the time, so we went to the bedroom and closed the door. Dana told me that she was feeling sick and had missed her period. She didn't know what to do and thought she was pregnant. She was devastated because she was already ranked in the nation in track and expected to be a star athlete at the Junior Olympics. Immediately, all my thoughts about what happened with Cecilia came back to my memory. I couldn't believe this was happening again. We used protection. How in the world could she be pregnant? I didn't love this girl. She was just another piece for me to satisfy a horny college male's sexual craving. I didn't have any feelings for her at all. I never even called this girl. My response made her furious and upset because I asked her who else she was sleeping with. I said there was no way she was pregnant and that it could be mine because I used protection. I told her she needed to figure it out because I wasn't the one.

After she started cursing me out, Amy had to step in and try to calm her down. Finally, Amy got her to leave and asked me what had happened. I told her, and Amy was mad at me again. Like a big sister, she told me I needed to stop messing around with all of these girls before something serious happened. Deep down, I knew Amy was right, but I seemed to be getting hurt all my life, so now it was time for me to do the hurting. I didn't care about these girls. I just wanted to eat, have fun, get free clothes, money, and party. I didn't care about school, started not to care about track, and now I was beginning to get around the wrong crowd. It was like my life was starting to take a turn for the worse, and there was nothing I could do about it. I wasn't going to stop. I was a college athlete. I made it when people didn't believe in me. I continuously proved people wrong about me, and I always had to fend for myself. I didn't need anyone or anything to tell me what to do or how to run my life. A few weeks later, Dana showed up at my apartment again. When I saw her through the peephole, my heart dropped. I opened the door, and she came in. She told me that she was only here for a minute.

She explained that she had a false alarm and wasn't pregnant. She told me that she couldn't mess with me anymore because her focus was on track, and if she were around me, she wouldn't be able to control her feelings, and we might slip up again. I was fine with this on the inside, but on the outside, I acted like I was shocked. Deep down, I didn't care and was relieved that she wasn't pregnant. This was the last time I saw Dana.

On a Saturday night, I got together with my friend Ricky because he was the man that knew where all the parties were taking place. After I picked Ricky up, we went cruising down Speedway Boulevard. We stopped at one of the sex stores that would have women dancing in a window. There were small rooms with curtains, and you would put a quarter in the slot, and they would dance for a couple of minutes in front of the glass. We used to get a kick out of this. After we were done, we headed to one of Ricky's friend house. Again, we were back on the Southside of Tucson. Everyone was wearing blue, black, and white. A lot of Mexicans and a few black guys were standing around in the yard drinking, and two guys were wrestling around the corner. I had a bad feeling in my stomach and knew something wouldn't go right again this night. One guy told Ricky and me that he wanted us to ride to the corner store with him to get some more beer. We were down with it because we loved to drink. Two guys got into the front of a black Chrysler Cutlass. The windows were tinted, so you could barely see in the car. They had gold Dayton rims, and the car was very nice. Ricky, me, and Ricky's friend got into the back of the car. We backed out of the driveway and headed to get some alcohol from the corner store. They were listening to Too Short, and we were all laughing and having a good time. The next thing I knew, the guy in the passenger seat spotted someone he had problems with and told the driver to turn around. They turned around, and as we started heading toward these people, I saw about five or six guys with red flannels and red rags in their back pockets. I knew this wasn't going to be good. The car started to slow down, and I saw the passenger lift his gun, aim out the window, and randomly start firing shots toward these guys! After about 30 seconds and seeing these guys take off running, the driver sped off, and we returned to the house.

I tried to play cool and act like it was nothing, but my heart was racing inside my chest, and once again, another episode where I could have gone to jail. If these guys had shot back, I could have possibly been shot and killed. This was it! I knew if I didn't do something and do it fast, my luck would run out, and I would either be behind bars or sitting in jail or prison. I wasn't a bad kid, but I made bad choices and put myself in some crazy predicaments that could have ruined my life for good. I could lose my scholarship and get kicked out of college. Then what would I do? I returned to my apartment that night, thinking I had to get myself together and start doing things right. I had to stop going out so much and just settle down. I didn't need all of these girls. I had what used to be my best friend and girlfriend in Phoenix. I could drive to see her, and she could still come to see me. We talked on the phone, and I told her that no matter what happened, I wanted to be with her once she graduated. I had some spare cash at the time, so I went out and bought us "Promise Rings." These rings represented not only our friendship but a promise that we would be together. I was living wild, crazy, and recklessly. It was time that I got back on track.

Around this time, Michelle let us know she was moving out within the next week or so. She was going to be moving in with her boyfriend. Shortly after she let us know this, Amy decided that she was going to transfer to a college in Phoenix so she could be closer to Marcus. Marcus claimed he wanted to get married to Amy soon. All this stuff was happening to me, and now I get two bombs dropped on my head at the same time. I didn't know what I was going to do. I wasn't making enough to stay at an apartment by myself. Amy said I could take over the lease, but I wouldn't be able to pay it by myself. I asked if other people I knew were looking for roommates, but I couldn't find anyone.

I went to school on Monday morning and received my progress reports for each class. I was failing 3 out of 5 classes that I was taking. I was about to be ineligible for track and wrestling once the reports hit my coach's desk. I had these reports in my hand, staring at them as I walked down the sidewalk toward the cafeteria. My life was over at this point. As I looked up, there was a table set up with a black cloth that said, "Be All You Can Be, In The Army." Two recruiters were standing there with pamphlets in their hands. I didn't know much about the Army or any other branch of service, but this may have been my way out of this pitfall I was finding myself in. I walked over to the table, and the recruiters asked me how I was doing. I told them I had just gotten my progress reports and was failing 3 out of 5 classes. I was about to be homeless because my roommates would be gone at the end of the semester, and I found myself around the wrong crowd more recently. They asked if I had ever been arrested, and I told them, "no." They asked if I had ever taken the ASVAB, and I couldn't remember. I knew we did something like that in high school, but I definitely didn't take it seriously. After we talked more about the Army opportunity, I signed up on the spot to take the ASVAB that weekend in Phoenix.

I continued to practice, work out, and go to class for the rest of the week. Once again, Friday night came, and Michelle and Amy wanted to have a going away party for Michelle. This was my other sister, so I couldn't turn down the opportunity. I knew I had to be up at 5 am to meet the recruiter to take this ASVAB. It was OK; I would party with them until about midnight and then get a few hours of sleep. That's the worst lie I told myself that night. We had about 20 people over at the apartment, drank all night, and again, Dominique was in my sight. We hooked up again late that night, and I didn't get to bed until around 3:30 am. Luckily, Dominique stayed over that night and was the one that woke me up at 4:30 am so I could get dressed and meet the recruiter. I was about 10 minutes late. I pulled up, parked my car, and he had me get into the car with him. I told him I stayed up all night partying and asked if it was wise for me to take this test. Of course, he told me not to worry about it. On our ride to Phoenix, I asked him how long it would take me to get out of Tucson and go to Basic Training. He told me it would be 1-2 months. That was perfect timing because I could be gone before Amy left, and I would be homeless. We got to the MEPS (Military Entrance Processing Station), and I woke up. I fell asleep on the way there, trying to get all the rest I could. We went into the building, and they did some random checks, making sure I didn't have flat feet, could squat down, bend over, and was healthy enough to join the Army. The recruiter took me to a room with some other potential recruits, and we all took the ASVAB. I can't remember the details of the test as I was not in my right mind at the time. I remember calling my mom and asking her what the job of a Unit Supply Specialist was because she did the same thing. She was shocked that I was up there and told me it was a good field. The other options were: truck driver, food service, big wheel mechanic, and, of course, infantry. I told them I would like to be a Unit Supply Specialist as a potential MOS (Military Occupational Specialty). After we finished, the recruiter drove me back to Tucson and told me that I should stay in touch with them and do physical training to ensure that I was in good shape for basic training. I told him I was already an athlete and didn't need to get in shape. When I got back to the apartment, I told Amy and Michelle about my experience, and they were shocked that I followed through with it.

CHAPTER 19

Be All That You Can Be

A FEW WEEKS LATER, I received a call from the Army recruiter. He told me that I had passed everything and would be able to ship out to basic training on February 27th, 1996. I was excited but, at the same time, very nervous. Everything was getting real and moving really fast. The hard part would be when I had to go to school that day and let my coach know I would be leaving for the military. How would I tell him this news, especially when I was on a full-ride scholarship? This was going to be hard, but it needed to be done. I had to make a drastic change in my life in order to move on and move forward. When I arrived at school that morning, I literally had to talk myself into getting out of the car and going to my coach's office. It took me about 30 minutes, but I headed straight to the gym once I got out. I walked to his office and knocked on the door. My heart was pounding, and everything inside me told me not to go through with it. Coach opened the door, and I told him that I had some news I needed to share with him. He greeted me, as he always did, with a smile and a firm handshake.

He told me to come into his office and have a seat. I walked in and slowly sat down in the chair. I told Coach about everything I was going through. I told him about my roommates leaving, almost getting shot a few times, getting around the wrong crowd lately, all of the girls I was messing with, failing my classes, and everything else happening in my life. After I explained everything, I told him I spoke with one of the Army recruiters on campus and told him about my trip to Phoenix to take the ASVAB. At this point, he sat up in his chair and started to look puzzled. I explained that the Army recruiter told me I would be going to basic training on February 27th, which was less than a month away. I hoped he would understand, but Coach had turned "red." He was angry, but I could tell he was trying to hold it in and stay professional. He asked me if I understood how much the school invested in me for a full-ride scholarship and if I left, I would have to pay the money back. I didn't know, and at this point, no matter what he said, he couldn't convince me to stay. I had to move on and do what I needed to do. The Army was going to help me become a man, give me a place to sleep, provide me with a paycheck, a job, and give me food. If I stayed in college, I didn't know what my future would hold. Every time I tried to get on the right track, the weekend would come, and all the rules I made for myself would go out the window.

Coach told me he understood but disagreed with my decision. He said I was making the biggest mistake of my life and to go to the counselor's office and let them know I was dropping out. I got up and told him I was sorry for wasting his time. Then I turned around and walked out the door, gently closing it behind me. As I walked back through the gym, I could only think, "Was this the biggest mistake of my life? Is he right? What am I doing?" As I walked toward the cafeteria back to where I usually parked, I saw Veronica standing by the soda machines. As I got closer, she smiled, but I didn't feel like being bothered by anyone at the time. She asked me what was wrong. I told her what had just happened, and she was shocked. She told me that, although it was a big decision, she thought I would do well. She also said it would be good for me to get away from this city and start a new life. There was nothing in this city worth staying for, and I would be successful once I left. I thanked her for her encouraging words. She gave me a big hug and told me good luck in the real world and that she knew I would make something great out of myself. I told her goodbye and to stay out of trouble. I thanked her for her friendship and began walking towards my car. Once I got to my car, I leaned back in my seat, closed my eyes, and still couldn't believe all of this was really happening.

I drove back to the apartment and remembered sitting in the apartment complex for about two hours, reflecting on my entire life up to this point. Amy pulled in and parked next to me. By this time, I had about 4 Coronas while sitting in the car. Amy got out, looked at me, and knew something was wrong. She walked to the passenger side of the car, got in, and started yelling at me like a big sister. She asked me what I was doing and why I was drinking in the middle of the day like an alcoholic. This girl really cared for me like her brother. I was very grateful to her, and although she could be rough on me, I explained everything that had happened earlier that day. She comforted me and hugged me while telling me everything would work out for the better. I would always let Amy hear the new raps that I would write in my free time, and she reminded me that she always thought I would end up being a rapper anyway. We both laughed, and she made me get out of the car and go upstairs to the apartment. Later that night, she cooked for us, which she rarely did. Most of the time, it was just for her. She made me cook my food. She would always remind me that I wasn't her boyfriend, Marcus. I thanked her for being a great friend and told her I would miss her. We always looked out for each other, no matter how mad we were at each other. We were truly family and would never forget each other.

It was two days before I had to ship out to basic training. It was a Friday, and Amy and Michelle had planned a big going-away party for me. There were about 30 people that came to the party, including some people I hadn't seen since high school. Once she told Max, Anthony, Mike, and a few others, the word started to spread that I was going into the military. Everyone was having a great time, reflecting on all the good and bad times we had back through high school until now. Gabe was making us laugh as he was still trying to hook up with Amy. Amy was always freaked out by him and kept giving me a look to come to her rescue. All I could do was laugh and continue to drink with all of my friends that came out. Everyone kept telling me they couldn't believe I signed up for the Army and that it was going to be interesting to see if I made it or not. I told them I couldn't believe I signed up for the Army either, but at least I was in great shape for basic training. As the night continued and people started leaving, there were only a few of us left, holding on to those final hours. Max, Amy, Dominique, Michelle, and me. We all continued to tell crazy stories and reflect on our memories of each other. When I looked at these guys, I had a love for them that I couldn't explain. They were some great friends, and I wouldn't trade them for the world. I was glad I met Amy and Michelle. I was glad that I met Max a few years ago. Although we didn't hang out as much after we graduated, we always picked up right where we left off.

We all eventually fell asleep around 5 am that morning. I remember Dominique waking me up because she had to leave. She hugged me and told me to be safe and to take care of myself. She said she would miss me and never forget our crazy times together. I told her to make sure she got a good guy that would treat her right and take care of her. She laughed and joked about there not being any of those types of guys in Tucson. I walked her to her car and told her to be safe and that no matter what life threw at her, she was a strong girl and could handle it. She agreed as she got into her car. I shut her door. She started the car and slowly backed out of the parking space. She waved bye through the side of her glass window, and this would be the last time I would ever see Dominique.

As I began packing my things and getting ready to leave the next day, I started reflecting on all the good and bad memories I had of this place. This next season of my life was going to either make or break me. I wasn't used to being bossed around and hated it when someone spoke loudly or yelled at me. It would remind me of when I was a little kid and heard my biological dad yelling at my mom while he physically beat her. How was I going to be able to handle someone in my face barking commands, yelling, and calling me everything but a child of God? I would have to prepare mentally before I headed into basic training if I wanted to make it through the course. I had no other choice but to succeed and was willing to do whatever it took to make it. As I woke up that next morning, everything was about to get real. I grabbed my bags and told Amy bye one last time. I told her to take care and thanks for everything. As tough as Amy was, she broke down and started crying. I hugged her and told her to be strong. I reminded her to keep in touch, or I would hunt her down when I got out of training. We laughed, and I headed down the steps to where Max was waiting in the parking lot. He asked what I would do with my car, which we called "Turbo." I told him I would leave it there because I didn't need it anymore. This was a great car, and we had some great times. It got us all around the state of Arizona. Half the time, we were drunk, and I don't even remember getting home, but good ol' Turbo brought us back safely. I still owed $1200 on the car due to the interest rate I received being so high, but now that I was going to the Army, I didn't need it anymore. We both waved bye and laughed at good ol' Turbo, and as we pulled out in his car, he asked me if I was ready. I remember saying that we would find out in due time. We headed out of the parking lot and proceeded to the airport. We reminisced some more on the short drive to the airport, which seemed like one of the shortest rides I had ever been on. Everything was moving so fast, and it was time for me to check in. I gave Max a dap and told him thanks for everything. He told me to take care of myself. I walked into the busy airport and checked in for my flight to Columbia, South Carolina, as my basic training would be at Ft. Jackson, South Carolina.

CHAPTER 20
Basic Training

WHEN I ARRIVED at the Columbia, SC airport, there were a lot of other young guys that looked like me. They were young, some fat, some skinny, some with long hair, some with short hair, and nobody looked like the Army guys I saw on TV. We were all waiting with our luggage for a nice van or bus to pick us up so we could arrive at the nice training facility that the recruiter gave me the impression of. He said that we would get free breakfast, lunch, and dinner and stay in nice dorms. It would be like a regular job, and I would have to just listen to the guys telling me what time work started and where I had to be every day. As we were all sitting together, laughing and joking, two old white school buses pulled in. These guys with large round hats got off the bus smiling and greeting all of us with a smile. They asked if we were there for basic training, and when we all said "yes," they asked if we needed assistance with our luggage. We all looked at each other and smiled because these guys were very nice. They didn't get anyone to help with our luggage, but they politely guided us to the buses and told us to sit anywhere we wanted. This basic training that everyone was talking so badly about was about to be a piece of cake. It wasn't anything like what they mentioned in the movies or from hearsay.

Once we got on the bus, we all sat down and started laughing and joking about how easy this would be. We couldn't believe the lies people told about these nice guys with the large, round hats called Drill Sergeants. They were very polite and welcoming. As we sat there waiting for everyone to get on the bus, we heard the bus start behind us, then our bus started. We were excited to get to the new location that would be our new home for the next eight weeks. I remember the bus being loud as everyone was laughing, listening to music, and getting to know each other. All of a sudden, out of nowhere, three Drill Sergeants stormed up the steps. One moved quickly to the back, one towards the middle, and the last one was in the front. Next, it was something I had never experienced in my life. These nice gentlemen turned into the worst demons that I had ever seen. Their faces were scrunched up as they began barking loud commands at everyone. Spit was flying out of their mouths, and they were ensuring to get in everyone's faces, yelling, screaming, and cursing at us. They were talking about our mothers, grabbing our bags in our laps, yanking them out of our hands, and throwing them across the bus. They told us, "Welcome to hell," and that they would be our nightmare for the next eight weeks, if we even survived that long. I was still shocked and tried not to make eye contact with any of these guys so they wouldn't come toward me. As we pulled out of the airport parking lot, they told us to put our heads in between our laps and that we better not look up. Everyone quickly did it. I still remember this skinny Caucasian kid next to me started crying. I didn't want to say anything to him because they also told us if they caught us talking, that would be the last word that ever came out of our mouths.

This seemed to be the longest bus ride I had ever been on. I couldn't believe what was happening and started thinking if I had made the right decision or not. How was I going to handle this for the next 8 weeks? This was crazy and ridiculous. Once we pulled up to where we would get off, called the "Reception," the Drill Sergeants started barking at us to hurry up and exit the bus. We all moved as fast as we could, bumping and pushing each other until we got to the open parking lot, where we would have to get into something that they called a "formation." We had no clue what they were talking about, so more yelling, cursing, and spitting came flying from these guys' mouths until we finally figured it out. This was the longest night ever. We would proceed to do push-ups, side straddle hops (jumping jacks), and run around the bus until they got tired. In reality, I think they were trying to see how many of the fat kids they could make throw up so they could brag later that evening amongst each other. The physical stuff didn't bother me because I was coming out of college, running track and wrestling, so I was in great shape, especially compared to 99% of these other guys. After the emotional and physical torture, they finally assigned us to a room at Reception and let us know that we would be there for about one week while we were in-processing, awaiting our assigned company.

This was the last time we would see these guys for a while. We went to sleep that night, and I remember hearing people snoring, tossing, and turning as if they had just run a marathon. I lay there looking at the bottom of the bunk bed above me, wondering what would come next. Early the next morning, another guy came into our room and woke us up. He told us he wasn't a Drill Sergeant and would be with us for the next week as we went through some paperwork, shots, and uniform issues. He wasn't yelling like the Drill Sergeants. He explained where the "Chow Hall" was located and what times we needed to be where. Again, we were all confused and thought this was another trick. While we were in Reception, they gave us a book with the basic information that we would need to learn for Basic Training. It included military rank and basic commands. We were expected to learn this the week before we were shipped off to the Basic Training Site. This place was very relaxed, and we went and came throughout the chow hall and our building without anyone bothering us. During this week, we received what seemed to be like a thousand shots, filled out paperwork in case something happened to us, and received a bank account from Ft. Jackson Federal Credit Union. We had a lot of time on our hands, and some of us guys connected and stayed together. We would write raps and spit our bars to each other while another guy would b-box. We had a disposable camera, and we all posed with our shirts off in our new camouflage BDUs like we were hardcore gangsters. You couldn't tell us anything. One of the funniest moments was when it was time to go through the haircut line. Some guys had long hair, and after the barber was done, they were completely bald. I always had short hair, so it didn't affect me. Some of these guys didn't take it too well and were shocked. This was hilarious.

The day finally came when it was time for us to ship off to the actual training. Once again, these Drill Sergeants came barking commands at us, yelling for us to get on the bus. Everyone had their green duffle bags strapped to their backs, and we were in our new BDUs. This time it didn't seem as bad, but I think we were just over the initial shock that came out of nowhere, so it didn't affect us as much. We pulled up to our company and exited the bus as the Drill Sergeants were still barking at us. Now we were fully under their control. They made us lie on our backs and do what they called flutter kicks; front, back, go's; and, of course, push-ups. Front, back, go's was where we would do push-ups when they called out "front," flutter kicks when they called out "back," and running in place very fast when they called out "go." This went on for about 45 minutes to an hour. Finally, we got to put our stuff up in the open bays where we would be staying. We were assigned bunks and lockers. The showers were open-bay, and everything was very clean. I could only imagine who would be doing the cleaning. After our stuff was put up, they took us to the chow hall, and now we were rushed to get our food, unlike at the reception station we just came from. We had all day to eat. As soon as we sat down and took one bite, the Drill Sergeant yelled for us to get up and put our trays away. Needless to say, over time, we learned to eat very fast. One of the highlights I remember was this thing called a "PT Test." This was known as a "Physical Fitness Test." This test would determine whether we were within Army physical fitness standards. The test consisted of push-ups, sit-ups, and a 2-mile run within a certain amount of time.

We took the PT test, and I missed maxing out the test by 1 point. I received a 299 out of 300 at the time. It seemed like now I was on the Drill Sergeants' good side. They weren't yelling at me as much, and some of us got special privileges if we did well on our tests. They trained us in hand-to-hand combat, firing an M16 rifle, first aid, military rank structure, setting up a one-man tent in the field, making fighting positions, patrols, and many more necessary skills for survival in war. Every morning we would wake up for PT training at 0500 hrs. In an hour, we would run about 3–4 miles and do a variety of exercises. When we weren't at the range qualifying or learning a new skill, we didn't have much downtime. They would make us clean the barracks. Our beds would have to be made in a certain way that was taught to us, and our wall lockers had to be in order. We were being stripped of everything we thought we knew and re-programmed into the soldiers they wanted us to become. As time passed, more males and females started to notice each other. The female barracks were above us, and now that we were used to our daily routines, our focus shifted to impressing the girls. A couple of us would claim which girl we wanted to get with, and we would chase after them. I remember, during our last couple of weeks, we would sneak into the stairwell and meet halfway. I met with one particular girl I found cute, and we would be in the stairwell, kissing and playing with each other's private parts to satisfy our urges. I still cannot believe we didn't get caught and even got bold enough to sneak them into our bays late at night.

During our last two weeks of Basic Training, we would conduct a 12-mile road march, qualify for our M16, NBC chamber, and pass our PT test one final time. Since we were sneaking around with the females late at night, some of us were always tired the next morning. On the morning of the road march, I was exhausted as I had only had about 2 hours of sleep. We lined up and began our road march. The physical part was easy for me. Even during the beginning stages of Basic Training, I was in the push-up position so much that I fell asleep. During this road march, we were around our 9-mile mark, and I couldn't take it anymore. My eyes were getting heavy, but my body was still going. I remember closing my eyes while I continued marching. One of the Drill

Sergeants was watching me the entire time. I walked for about 200 meters with my eyes closed while staying in formation. I opened my eyes right in time and saw a huge pothole that I would have stepped right into if I hadn't woken up. The Drill Sergeant laughed and told me, "You woke up right on time, Private!" Our other requirements, such as the M16 qualification and PT test, were easy. I excelled at both of these requirements and received a PT Fitness Badge Award to wear on my PT uniform for excelling and passing the extended scale of the scoring requirements. Next up was the NBC Chamber. I have been claustrophobic since my uncle stuffed me in that big ball when I was little. I wasn't fond of wearing this gas mask. We would have to go into the gas chamber with this mask on and take it off while breathing this gas, and we would not be able to exit until the Drill Sergeant let us. Somehow, I made it right on time and was about to crack when the Drill Sergeant opened the door, and we all ran out. People were puking, spitting, snot running down our faces, gagging, and coughing like we were about to die. I could tell that this was one of the Drill Sergeants' favorite events. They filmed and laughed hysterically at all of us. It was finally over, though. The only thing we had in front of us was graduation. The Drill Sergeants even started to talk to us like normal people. I remember a Drill Sergeant challenging me to a sit-up competition. Everyone gathered around us, and all my classmates knew I would win, so they were cheering. Our morale was up, and we were hyped. Everyone got in a circle, and the rules were that we would go 1 for 1 until the first person quit. Needless to say, once we started, within about 2 minutes into the competition, the Drill Sergeant gave up. Everyone cheered, and the Drill Sergeant congratulated me and left.

This wasn't so bad anymore, but now it was time to leave. We got reprogrammed, I made new friends, and I passed the course. I did it! No looking back now. Advanced Individual Training (AIT) was in front of me. We lined up on the field, and we all looked very good in our Class A uniforms. We had one ribbon and our marksmanship qualification badge on our uniform. Our shoes were extremely black and shiny, and we were ready to march across that field. As we lined up, we stood at attention with our old green Class A hats canted to the side, our heads straight, and our eyes forward. The Drill Sergeant yelled out the command, "Forward, March!" We marched past all of the family and friends in the bleachers as they cheered for us. This was one of the proudest moments I have ever felt. Many families were there. However, I didn't have anyone in the crowd. But it was fine because I was used to not having any family at my events. My friends always had their mom, dad, uncles, cousins, etc., at the football, wrestling, and track meets. Not me. I can count on one hand how many times my parents came to any of my games. This would be no different. It bothered me for about a minute until I snapped back to my senses and realized how far I had come. I was now in the United States Army and heading to AIT, where I would learn my actual job training and specialty. Basic Training was now complete!

CHAPTER 21

Advanced Training

AS EVERYONE SAID their goodbyes at the end of the Basic Training graduation, we told each other to stay the course and finish strong. We learned how to help one another and grew together as a big family. This was my new family. Some of us would still be together as we had the same job, which was called a MOS. My training would be in Fort Lee, Virginia as a 92Y Unit Supply Specialist. I would have to attend this training for approximately 8 weeks before I was assigned to an actual Army unit. It was Friday, and our training would begin on Monday. I got on my flight from Columbia, SC, and headed to Richmond, VA. Once I landed, there was a shuttle bus that would take everyone coming in for training to Ft. Lee. We boarded the shuttle bus and headed to the new base where we would be for our next training. This wasn't nearly as bad as the beginning of Basic Training. Once we arrived, the Drill Sergeants assigned us to our new open bay rooms. We could walk to the PX, which was a store similar to a Wal-Mart. The PX was about a mile down the road. We went and got some real food from the food court and bought some new clothes. We were allowed to wear regular clothes on the weekend, and we would get passes to leave the base as well! This was bound to be a great time because we had more freedom and were no longer in Basic Training.

Monday morning came, and this was our very first day. The Drill Sergeants were still a little strict but nowhere near what we were used to. They talked to us like people and assigned us roles such as 1SG, Platoon SGT, Squad Leader, Admin, PT Duty, and more. Now we had some real responsibilities that we would be responsible for performing while in AIT. We wouldn't keep these duties the entire time, but they would rotate to a new person throughout the week. Every morning we would wake up, conduct PT, shower, get dressed, and march to the chow hall. We had more time to eat, so we could actually taste our food now, and nobody was barking at us to hurry up. After eating, we would return and get our books and book bags. It was similar to a college-style environment, just more organized. While each platoon was lined up before we would all march together, each platoon had a motto that we would yell out. Because I rapped, I came up with our platoon's motto, and we won it a few times, earning us extra privileges for the week. We could stay out one hour later or leave one hour earlier for the weekend.

When we went to our class, we had instructors that weren't Drill Sergeants but rather regular military personnel assigned to teach us our job. For the most part, these soldiers were pretty cool and spoke to us like human beings as well. We would go over the jobs we would conduct once we got to our actual unit. They explained that we needed to pay attention because sometimes, when we arrive at our units, there may not be anyone there but us. The commander will expect us to know our jobs and that our roles as Unit Supply Specialists are among the most important within the company. They explained that everyone leaned on us and we had one of the best MOSs in the entire

Army. Of course, we were all thrilled and excited, but we were also nervous. They were teaching us our jobs. We would take tests, and if we passed, we would move on to the next subject. Some of the subjects were very easy, and some were a little harder. We learned about the forms we would use in our jobs and how to properly fill them out. We learned various scenarios and how to properly deal with them when they arise. They taught us how to be armorers and how to properly fill out the inspection reports for the arms room. Everything we did was at the basic knowledge level and just enough so we could succeed and not go to our units blind. We only had approximately 8 weeks to learn this stuff, so we were moving fast and learning a different skill almost daily.

We all looked forward to the weekends because we could leave and get hotel rooms off base. We had a connection that would get us some alcohol, and once we were dismissed for the weekend, everyone quickly changed clothes, packed, and hopped in the closest taxi to get off base. Our first stops would be the hotel to get the rooms we would share, and then we would pile up in the taxi and eat at the mall. If we felt really good, we would go to the local Red Lobster or Applebee's. Some of the girls in our class would ask us what we were going to do for the weekend, and they would ask if they could meet up with us. We had a lot more freedom, so we told them yes. They would have their own hotel rooms at the same location, but it seemed like we always ended up in the same rooms, hugged up with each other. As the night went on, we weren't dumb, so we partied, but we didn't make much noise. We had alcohol, and the last thing we wanted was to get caught and kicked out of AIT. We got this far, so we couldn't jeopardize everything we have accomplished thus far. Everyone was on the same page, and we had our little clicks. There were about six of us that hung out together. We were known as the more "squared away" soldiers, and the girls gravitated toward us. We were young, nice looking, with great bodies, and now we were getting great paychecks. This was the life. At the hotels on the weekends, the girls would get with us, and we would all share some drinks, listen to music, and talk about our experiences, hopes, and futures. We didn't know where we would be stationed at this point, so some of the guys would talk about some of the various assignments they had heard about. Nobody wanted to go to Korea or Ft. Drum. We didn't know much about the other duty stations other than what the Drill Sergeants would tell us and where they'd been stationed. We had become a family in Basic Training and had now met some people we considered part of our team. We were hoping that a majority of us would get stationed together.

The time came on one sunny day in June when we were all about to find out where we would be stationed after graduating. The Drill Sergeants had our platoon in front of the Mighty Mike headquarters building. We were sitting down on the grass, waiting patiently for the Drill Sergeant to come back with our assignments in hand. He walked up, and we were all eagerly waiting as he handed out the papers in his hand. He called our name, and we answered loudly, "Here, Drill Sergeant!" My name was called, and hoping that I had somewhere good, I anxiously grabbed my paper and sat back down. Once I opened the folded paper, it had some basic information, such as my name and social security number. Halfway down the paper, in bold black letters, it read, "447th Signal Battalion, Fort Gordon, GA." At the time, I was confused and kind of upset because I didn't want to go to Georgia. I wanted to go to Fort Bragg, NC, and eventually to Airborne School. I was even thinking about becoming an Airborne Ranger and attending a Ranger Course. My Drill Sergeant asked us what our assignments were. Some people had Germany, Ft. Stewart, Ft. Hood, Ft. Bragg, Ft. Drum, and many had Korea. There were only two of us with Fort Gordon, GA. Nobody wanted to go to Korea. This was one of the worst places you could go at this time. The weather was cold and miserable, everyone had a curfew, and they stayed in the field doing training all the time. This was the definition of the real Army. We didn't want any part of that. The people that got Korea were mad, and their morale dropped as they had nothing to look forward to. I remember my Drill Sergeant asking me where I was going, and I told him Fort Gordon, GA. He told me I was very lucky and that this was one of the best places to be stationed. I still didn't believe him, but oh well, it was definitely better than Korea any day.

During the rest of the time in AIT, we would take our mattresses off the beds and form a wrestling pit. I was only 150 lbs at the time, but I also used to wrestle. This made me one of the better wrestlers in our class. We would have tournaments, and I would always win easily over the other guys in my platoon. There was only one guy I would have trouble wrestling with, and he weighed about 190 lbs. He was 40 lbs heavier than I was. However, he would barely beat me when we wrestled. There were a couple of times I would beat him, and he would give up. However, he got the best of me most of the time. The girls would watch us wrestle, and all the guys would place bets on who would win. It was funny because before they saw me in action, I wasn't picked as one of the ones to win. However, after they watched my first match against one of the supposedly tougher kids in our class, their whole perception changed. Many of these guys didn't know I wrestled in high school and didn't know I went to college on a scholarship for wrestling and track. I tried to keep most of this stuff to myself. There were a couple of guys I was close with that I shared my story with, and they shared theirs as well. These were the only guys that knew I was pretty athletic. However, some people could tell because I got the PT Award in Basic and would continue to do so in AIT.

The time came when it was time for us to graduate and once again move on. We would all part ways soon and head to our first duty stations. Our Drill Sergeants always told us to keep in touch and care for each other. It was our last weekend, and we were on a pass. There was a specific girl I had my eye on and was waiting until the last weekend to make my move. She knew I liked her because we would always flirt during class and talk a lot of smack to each other about what we would do if we were alone. The time was finally about to come when we would get the opportunity to be alone. Many of the guys had their girls they were hooking up with for the last weekend, so nobody was planning on partying and getting rooms together. This last weekend would be with the girls we wanted to hook up with the whole time while we were in AIT. I got dressed and went outside, patiently waiting for this girl I liked to come out as well. I was talking to one of my friends who was heading to the hotel for the weekend. He asked me what I was going to be doing, and I told him I was waiting for this girl. While we were talking, she came out, and while she was walking, a Drill Sergeant from another platoon pulled up and called her over. He had a red Ford Expedition with tinted windows and chrome rims. He always showed off his sound system. I was still talking to my boy, and we looked toward the truck. The next thing I knew, she opened the door and got in. They pulled off, and I was shocked. Drill Sergeants weren't supposed to be messing around with privates. They could get into big trouble. Evidently, they didn't care. I wouldn't see her for the whole weekend and ended up hanging out with some of the other guys at the club they had for us on post. It was one of the most boring weekends I had while there, and I was salty about the whole situation. That Sunday, I didn't speak to the girl; she could tell something was wrong. She asked me what was wrong, and I told her to go talk to her Drill Sergeant friend and not worry about what I was doing. We didn't talk much the rest of that week, and when graduation came on Friday, I was ready to get to my duty station.

After graduation, we were all given 30 days' leave time to go back home and visit our friends and family before going to our official duty stations. I was excited to see everyone. I had been gone for almost five months, and now I was a brand new person. I was more mature now, and I was an official soldier in the United States Army. Max had his own place in Tucson, and before I got there, I made arrangements to stay at his place while I was at home. I got on my flight, and there were so many people I wanted to see when I returned so they could see the new me. Once I landed, Max picked me up. It was like we never missed a beat. We picked up right where we left off. He told me there was a party that night and many people were going to be there, including many friends I already knew. I was excited. We went back to his house for a couple of hours, drank some beers as we always did, got dressed, and headed out. Once we got to the party, it seemed like everyone I knew was there. Word got around that I was back home, and everyone wanted to see me and hear about my experience. I remember telling everyone how crazy Basic Training was and all of the craziness we went through. After a few more beers, I even demonstrated some patrol techniques to my friends. Later that night, I met another girl that I had seen at the party all night. I noticed she was looking at me smiling, but I was so caught up in telling my story that I didn't pay much attention to her. After everything slowed down, we crossed paths outside the parking lot and began talking for about an hour or so. We were both tipsy and feeling each other. The next thing I knew, we were back at Max's house, and I was hooking up with another female.

The next morning, I went to see my mom and Joe to tell them about my experience. I also went to see Rosemary and Gabe and told them I was doing well. I spent time with everyone and stayed at all of their houses for a couple of days each before heading back to Tucson with Max. It felt like I was coming home from prison, so I wanted to party as much as possible. Nothing was going on where my mom and Rosemary lived, so I was ready to get back to Tucson as soon as possible. I spoke with Monique on the phone, and we were going to meet to see each other. By this time, I knew we were done, but we were still friends and had our promise rings. The way I lived and the wild lifestyle I was engulfed in, the promise rings didn't mean much more than a friendship now. When we met, we discussed my living in Georgia as she was still finishing her senior year in high school. It was like she already knew we wouldn't last because there was a whole other world out there that I was now exploring. We went to her house in Phoenix while her parents were gone, made out, and were intimate with each other, but this was going to be the last time we saw each other, and we both knew it. We were sad, but at the same time, we knew reality had hit. We agreed to keep the promise rings we gave each other, and as time was winding down, we said our goodbyes, and I rode back to Tucson with Max. We partied one last night before it was time for me to return to reality and go to my first assignment. We had a great time, and I was able to see some of my friends that I hadn't gotten to see before I left. I told everyone that I would miss them and to be safe. That next morning, I woke up and knew my life was about to become even more real than it was. I was going off on my own, and now I was becoming my own man.

CHAPTER 22

Stay The Course

I WAS VERY NERVOUS upon arriving at Fort Gordon, GA. I didn't know anybody; this was my first duty station. I was already used to doing things on my own my whole life, but this seemed a little different. I would have to check in at a certain building and give them a copy of my orders. The taxi knew exactly where to go, and it was evident that he was used to doing this. He dropped me off at the main building on Fort Gordon, where everyone had to check in when they were new to post. This would be where you provide all of your information, and upon checking the database, they would assign you to your company. Upon my arrival, the person to whom I was supposed to give my orders and folder took them and called out my new company. She told me they would arrive shortly and that I should wait in the seating area. A shuttle bus arrived, and the Staff Duty NCO picked me up. He took me to my new location, where I would be assigned and would begin to work as soon as I in-processed. I remember seeing my supervisor, who was an African American male. He was an SSG, also known as an E-6. He was talking to me and told me that after he processed some paperwork, he would take me to the barracks and get me a room. I let him know that I understood. He seemed very busy, and he finally told me to get in his car when he finished. We drove over to these buildings that looked a little older but were better than the buildings we were staying at in Ft. Lee. He gave me my key, and I took my stuff to my room on the 2nd floor. I was about a quarter of the way down the hallway. I had my own room, and it looked like a mini apartment. This was going to be awesome. My NCO told me to unpack my stuff and get settled in. He gave me information about the location for PT, which would be at 6:30 the next morning. He said to ensure I was on time and in the proper uniform. I let him know that I understood. I unpacked all my items and remembered reflecting on how far I had come. I was now an official soldier and didn't know what to expect in the coming days.

The next morning, my alarm went off at 5:45 am, and I was anxiously waiting to go to PT. I knew about PT, and I was very good at it. I wanted to impress all the people I would be working with and show them that I was in excellent condition. The PT formation was about two blocks away at Barton Field. I arrived about 20 minutes early and thought I might be in the wrong location. A couple of cars pulled up, and a few people got out. They started walking over to the grass, and I proceeded to do the same thing. They asked if I was the new Private that had just arrived yesterday, and I said, "Yes." They started to talk amongst each other as more cars pulled up, and before I knew it, we had about 15 people standing around. This was nothing like Basic Training or AIT, as we formed up quickly there. Now everyone was moving slowly, like they really didn't want to be there, and when they formed up, people were talking and moving around. I wasn't used to this and was kind of confused. Were they supposed to be doing this? This wasn't what we learned in our training. Next, the PT instructor called out the command, "Extend to the left, march!" As we did in Basic and AIT, I yelled out loud as I proceeded to move fast, almost running the older man next to me over. This was crazy. It sounded like a bunch of old dead people, and they definitely moved like dead people. This couldn't be right. Once we started doing the exercises, everyone was getting tired quickly, and some didn't even finish. I continued to do what I knew was right. Next, we lined up in formation and marched to the dirt area on Barton Field, which was the track. We proceeded to jog slowly in formation. I just knew we were warming up and would take off a lot faster at any moment. This continued the entire time we ran for 30 minutes around Barton Field. I didn't even break a single sweat during our PT session. I thought to myself that this was a joke and couldn't believe we even wasted our time getting up early for this.

There was a Specialist (E-4) named Savannah. He had a small black sports car and asked if I wanted a ride back to the barracks. I told him, "Sure." I got into his car, and we pulled off. He asked me where I was from and seemed to be a pretty cool guy. He told me everything I learned in Basic and AIT is way different from the regular Army. He said that we wouldn't be doing all that craziness in the unit and that it would be a pretty chill assignment. I had no clue, as this was my first duty station, but now I was beginning to learn what it was like. Once we got to the barracks, I got dressed, walked to the chow hall, sat down, and ate my breakfast. I saw Savannah again, and he asked me if I wanted a ride to work. Of course I did. I didn't have a car because I left it in Tucson, and it was about a 2-mile walk to work. I went to the same location I was at the previous day, and the NCO said I wouldn't be working there. He told me that they were pulling me up to the Brigade S4. This was a higher headquarters than I was originally supposed to be working at. I got to my new office, and there were a lot of older people there. I can recall a few of the people that were there at the time, such as MSG Joyce, SSG Cooper, SGT Allen, SGT Brickhouse, and SGT Bunch. SGT Brickhouse was from the DC/Baltimore area; he was cool and down to earth. SGT Allen was from the islands. He was very scary and always kissed up to MSG Joyce. SGT Bunch was OK sometimes. She was a little on the weird side, a redhead with freckles, and was into a religion called Wicken. SSG Cooper was an older gentleman, bald, out of shape, down to earth, and cool. Later, I discovered he was also into music and loved his Primerica business. MSG Joyce was there for a short time, and she was really nice. A couple of weeks later, she was replaced by another MSG that came straight from the 2nd Infantry Division in Korea, where everyone dreaded going. He was very strict and always ensured we kept a neat, clean appearance with polished boots. He would inspect us every morning.

Of all the people, they put SGT Allen in charge of me. They told him to show me everything I needed to know. I was in charge of all of the work orders throughout the brigade, ensuring that the forms were turned in properly, and I had to make sure all of the paperwork was completed for the turn-in of broken and repaired equipment. Every so often, we would have to take the pick-up truck and conduct clean-up duties. This consisted of picking up trash and cigarette butts on the side of the road throughout the installation. I would also have to clean the office and bathroom every day before we got released for the day. My job wasn't too difficult and definitely didn't keep me busy. One day, we got a new NCO that came in to replace SGT Brickhouse as he was getting out of the Army. It was a cute, black, short female named SGT Lewis. SGT Lewis was cool, down to earth, and very squared away. She didn't talk down to me and always treated me with respect. SGT Brickhouse was into music and was a really good B-Boy dancer. The job I was in gave me plenty of time to start working on my craft of Hip Hop music. SSG Cooper even told me he would manage me because he had all kinds of connections across Augusta, GA, and could get me going. As time went on, I noticed that my job was very relaxed, which gave me plenty of time to do my extra-curricular activities.

During the weekend, I would hook up with some of the guys in the barracks, and we would go to some of the other barracks, drink, and then go out later. There was only one issue. I was underage at the time and couldn't get into most clubs. I could easily fix this issue because I remember a guy that worked in the admin office who would hook some military IDs up to make them look real and legit. He charged me $20 to get mine done, and now I could legally get into all the clubs. Once I saw how easy it was to do my ID, I knew a couple of other guys that needed it done, and while everyone was out of the office, I would go back and hook their IDs up. SSG Strahan and another guy had a car, so I would always roll out with them on the weekends. SSG Strahan was from Miami, Florida, and he was very fast. He wanted any girl he could get his hands on. He also loved his liquor. SSG Strahan was also into music, but more on the managing side. He swore he could get me shows and help me get my first tape out. He introduced me to another guy who we called DJ Humphrey. He was an SSG but stayed in housing with his wife and kids. We would always go to his house and hang out in his room. He would spin music, we would drink, and I would always freestyle. We had a great time, and now it seemed like everything was starting to fall into place. I would hang tight with Strahan, and we would hit every club in the city, from the NCO Club on post to Super C's, Millenium, and any other place that was open. Afterward, we always either hit up the Waffle House or Krystals.

Monday mornings were terrible because we always had to be at PT formation at 6:30 am. Half of the time, I would end up doing PT and running to formation to be on time because I would oversleep. Sometimes I made it on time, and sometimes I didn't. I was beginning to not care because these older people were wasting my time by having me come out to formation for PT. I could run faster and out-PT all of them, even when I was drunk and had no sleep. What was the purpose? I started not caring about my job and wanted to party and make music. I felt like the Army owed me something for what felt like a waste of my time. I would work out at lunch and almost joined the wrestling team with SGT Brickhouse. One day, we got a new Private straight from AIT, and her name was Celestine. I was happy because now I wasn't the lowest-ranking person in the company anymore. Celestine ended up living across the hall and a couple of doors down. We immediately connected because we were both Privates. She was an E-1; by this time, I was now an E-3. I remember her always trying to do the right thing and wanting to be squared away. Celestine was from the islands, light brown skinned, with long hair, and knew she was cute. Many guys would always try to flirt with her, but she didn't go for it. We were friends, so she would always let me hang out in her room, and sometimes she would come to mine. She would change in front of me, and I did all I could to control myself. A few times on the weekends, we would hook up, and I would stay in her room. I remember going out with Strahan and Rodney one night, and we got wasted, as we always did.

We didn't hook up with any girls, and I wanted to hook up with someone. Celestine was walking back from the laundry room with her clothes, and we started talking in the hallway. The next thing I knew, I was staying in her room that evening. She was a virgin, and I was the first guy she ever slept with. We ended up being together twice, and we both agreed that we couldn't do what we were doing anymore because we were in the same company. We had to work together sometimes, and she knew I wasn't serious about settling down with anyone then.

Savannah would knock on my door every morning to see if I needed a ride. I remember getting in his car one day and seeing a piece of hair on his seat. Savannah was seeing some crazy girl that would stalk him and never let him have any freedom. I told Savannah that I thought that old girl had forgotten a piece of her hair, and he turned bright red. Savannah was black, so it was funny when he turned bright red. We all clowned him from that day, but it was all good fun. At work, I continued to work on my music because my job was extremely slow. SGT Allen told me we had to go pick up trash that day, and we got into the red GMC truck. As we headed down the road, he told me to get out and pick up the cigarette butts on the side of the road. This made me angry because I didn't smoke, and why would I pick up someone else's cigarettes? SGT Allen started yelling at me, which made me even angrier because I didn't like anyone yelling or raising their voice at me. I told him to pull the truck over, and I was going to whoop his butt. He looked shocked and didn't say much. I continued to threaten him and told him that I wasn't joking. He immediately got scared and drove back to our office. He went straight to our new MSG's office and told him what had happened. Our new MSG brought me to the office, and I told him what I said because I didn't care at the time. They wrote me up and told me I would have to see the Brigade Sergeant Major. The Brigade SGM was the highest-ranking enlisted person in the Brigade. He was known as the Devil because of how evil he was. SGT Allen escorted me to his office and told me how I had to report to the Sergeant Major. Once it was time, I knocked on the door. He told me to enter, and I calmly walked in like I didn't have a care in the world. The SGM looked at SGT Allen and me and told me to get a parade rest. I blew air from my mouth, cocked my head to the side, and went to a relaxed parade rest position. SGM immediately blew a gasket and lost it. He started screaming and cursing and kicked me out of the office. He told SGT Allen to close the door, and all I could hear was him yelling at SGT Allen, tearing him apart with his words. SGT Allen came back out and took me back to work. I just knew I would get what they called an Article 15. Nobody ever wanted to get one of these. This was not good at all and would affect your military career. Days went by, and I never received Article 15. This was unheard of, and I am not sure what happened, but I was spared and given a second chance. They assigned SGT Lewis to me and told SGT Allen not to come near me. I think they knew I was kind of crazy and that SGT Allen was a weaker NCO than the rest of the team in the office.

SGT Lewis took me under her wing and immediately started explaining why I needed to do all the petty work they assigned to me. She spoke to me in a way I could understand and relate to. I now better understood why I needed to do certain things as a lower enlisted soldier. Once I got promoted, I wouldn't have to do these things anymore. I could supervise someone else and have more responsibility. More responsibility probably meant I wouldn't get into as much trouble anymore. I was getting better. However, now I was starting to get calls and letters from Monique. I hadn't seen or heard from her in forever. I was out on my own and chasing women with my homies. I still had feelings for Monique because we had been through so much together. However, I knew we would never get back together. I wanted to be her friend but didn't know how to separate what we had in the past. She was my best friend, and I couldn't just drop her like nothing. I was out in the streets pretty badly, almost as bad as before I joined the military. I was so bad that I even remember going to the NCO Club one night with Strahan and Rodney. I met a girl inside the NCO Club, and she took me back to her car and had sex with me. After we were done, we both got out of the car and went back in like we never knew each other. I continued to live on the wild side, and now that I was back in the music game, I was meeting even more people. One of the guys I met was a guy named Tyrone. We nicknamed Tyrone "Big Man." We ended up connecting immediately and would always make music together. Tyrone was also a good rapper, and we talked about forming a group and performing at the clubs together. We started getting more serious, and Big Man had connections with the studio where the best rappers in the city went to record. One of the main engineers' names was Buck T.

We would book studio time with Buck T; every time we went to the studio, it was like we were there all night. We would see guys come through, do their drug deals, sniff cocaine right there on the table, and smoke weed like it was nothing. I didn't care as long as we got our music recorded and it sounded good.

CHAPTER 23

The One

ALTHOUGH I WAS doing better at work and starting to get promoted, I was still hanging around with Strahan, Rodney, and now my new partner, Big Man. All Strahan and Rodney wanted to do was party and try to get me booked at some of the local clubs to show off my talents. Big Man connected with me, and we started making more music together in my barracks room to instrumentals by Mobb Deep, Wu-Tang Clan, Jay-Z, and many more. One night, the whole crew got together, and we planned on going to Super C's to perform at the weekly Talent Competition. We had performed there a few times before and won 2nd and 3rd place. This time I had my tape and was ready to perform. However, I didn't have any way to rewind the tape for the DJ so he could play my song and start it in the correct spot. Strahan and I were sitting in the parking lot trying to figure out how we could get my tape rewound for the competition. Out of nowhere, we see a light blue Hyundai Sonata car pull in with about 4-5 girls in it. I wasn't interested in talking to any girls at the moment; I was more concerned about getting this tape ready for the competition. This was my last and only hope, so I got out of the car and went up to the window. I leaned over by the car window and asked if I could use their tape deck to rewind my tape. The girls were laughing, and the main girl in the driver's seat rolled down the window. With a frustrated look, she asked me what I was saying. I was embarrassed and started laughing. Her girlfriends were tapping her, laughing, and nudging her to continue to talk to me. I told her that I needed to use her tape deck to rewind my tape due to the competition, and we began laughing and smiling at each other. I remember this girl asking me where my ring was and why I wasn't married. I told her that I hadn't found the right one yet. That was true, but the other part was I really wasn't looking, and marriage was nowhere on my mind.

I thought this girl was cute and got excited when she told me to come and get into her car. I got into the passenger seat, and we talked some more. I remember seeing her around before but never really spoke to her. Now we were talking, and it seemed like we were connecting. After I rewound my tape, we both got out of the car and went into Super C's. It was funny because this girl always wore dark sunglasses and ordered and drank Courvoisier straight. She would be on the small dance floor with her girlfriends, and they had some sort of dance routine to most of the down south booty shake music. We would have small talk in the club, and when I wasn't looking or went to the restroom, guys would try to get her attention. They would make their way to talk to her when we weren't together, but it always seemed like we ended up right back together, drinking, talking, and laughing again. I didn't like to dance much, but she definitely did. When Quad City DJs and Tootsie Roll came on, she quickly left me at the bar and would take over the dancefloor with her girlfriends, showing off their latest dance routines. I thought it was very cute and interesting at the time. She wasn't the type I would usually be interested in, but there was something different about her that drew me close and made me more interested in her. When the club closed at the end of the night, we would all rally up and eat at either the Waffle House or Krystals. These were the hot spots down south during the late night hours. It was like we didn't want the night to end. We exchanged numbers that night, and I wanted to fall asleep quickly so I could call this girl the next day. I wanted to get to know her a little better. When I met her, she seemed very down to earth, spontaneous, cute, with a great personality and fun to be with, which is a hard trait to find in a person. I thought it may have been too good to be true. However, time would tell, so I didn't want to get my hopes up.

As the next day came, I called her, and we spoke on the phone for a couple of hours. I invited her to come to my barracks and hang out with me for the night. I didn't have a car then, so I couldn't visit her. She accepted my invitation and later that day she arrived. When she arrived in the parking lot, she called me to tell me she was waiting. I was excited to see her, so I hurried down the steps to the parking lot where she was waiting. Miranda had on a headscarf and was dressed comfortably. In the back of my mind, I thought maybe she was testing me to see if I liked her for who she was and not how she looked. I didn't say anything about the scarf because I was still happy to see her. We talked outside for a while, and afterward went to get something to eat. Miranda still seemed to be very cool and down to earth. This was one girl I could definitely see myself hanging out with in the future. We talked about everything, including where I was from, her family, her job, my job, my music, and basically anything that would keep our conversation going so we could spend more time with each other. Miranda was working as a nurse when I met her. She helped the elderly at an Assisted Living Home and had that motherly loving spirit about her. We wouldn't see each other every day because of our work schedules. However, once the weekend hit, we would always link up. My friends, Strahan and Rodney, would get mad sometimes because all I would talk about was her and how I couldn't wait to see her again. Rodney and Strahan weren't trying to hear that. They wanted to see what women were out on the streets every night in Augusta and always wanted to hit the clubs. I would still go and hang out with them. However, I didn't find myself looking for that next victim as much. Instead, I always found myself linking up with Miranda as the night went along or we got close to heading home.

As time passed and we began hanging out more, Miranda stayed with me in my barracks room. She would cook on my hot plate, and we would spend all of our time together. We were becoming inseparable. I also began oversleeping and missing

Physical Fitness training. I was beginning to get into trouble at work from missing the formations and PT, but I didn't care because I fell more in love with Miranda as each day passed. We would stay up all night enjoying each other's company. We were like Bonnie and Clyde, willing to roll out whenever to wherever. We would often take off on the weekend to Florida with barely any money in our pockets, but we always had a great time. We were very spontaneous and willing to try just about anything. As time passed, Miranda began missing her shifts at work, and the managers could not get ahold of her, so they called her mom. One day, I heard a hard knock on my door, and from outside the door, I heard this voice say, "Miranda, are you in there? You need to open this door!" It was her mother! Being the honest and respectful man I am, I opened the door. I didn't realize Miranda was crawling under my bed, trying to hide! When the door opened and Mrs. Bullock walked in, I saw Miranda crawling from under my bed. This was one of the funniest things I have ever seen. However, with the look on Mrs. Bullock's face, I was not about to laugh. Miranda and her mom went outside and began arguing about her missing work. I felt bad, but I also didn't know she was always missing work to be with me. After arguing, Mrs. Bullock left, and Miranda returned to my room, explaining what had happened. I was upset that she didn't tell me she had stopped going to work because I didn't want to be the cause of her losing her job. Shortly after discussing the situation, she kept constantly getting messages on her pager. I thought she might have been dating another guy and wasn't telling me or being honest about everything, so I made her call the number back. The guy answered the phone and told me he just needed to ensure her car was in good shape and still running. Miranda tried to tell me not to fall for it, but

I didn't know the entire story or situation, so I agreed to meet him and show him the car was still in good shape. I drove the car to the meet-up location, and the guy got into the passenger seat. He lifted his shirt with a gun on his side and told me that the car was his once he sat in it. This was the repo man. He let me get all the stuff out of the trunk, and I had to take a taxi back to Fort Gordon. Once I got back, I walked in with all the items in my arms, and she was shocked. She was upset and told me I should've listened to her and not gone. Now we were both without a car but still spending a lot of time with each other. We would still have fun, but now we would catch the post taxi to go to the movies or different locations we wanted to go to on the weekend. It didn't seem like anything could stop us from seeing each other or having fun. Everything was going great until I got Miranda's call telling me she was pregnant. We were both young, crazy, and couldn't take care of another kid at this time. She didn't even take care of Shalita at the time. Miranda was 21, and I was 20 years old. We had barely grown ourselves. This was the first time we made one of our most devastating and worst decisions. We went to a Planned Parenthood location in Atlanta and aborted the baby. According to the nurse, it was a male. This was one of the worst feelings we have ever had and the hardest decision we have ever faced. We weren't married and didn't even know if we would be together, so how could we bring another kid into this world? Our decision pushed Miranda away from me as she was hurting inside, and neither of us knew how to handle the situation. Miranda grew up in a church, so she knew that abortion was against the will of God. I didn't have a clue and thought it was OK at the time, as I didn't want to bring a baby into this world, and we still liked hanging out, drinking, and partying all the time. All of the reasons we could not have a child were very selfish, and we did not realize it at that time.

The time came when I walked into my office and on my desk was a set of orders that had me PCS'ing to South Korea within the next 60 days. I was very upset and didn't want to leave. I found someone I enjoyed being around and began to fall in love with. Now I am being sent to another country! Not to mention, this would be the first time I would leave the country. I was a nervous wreck but wanted to spend as much time as possible with Miranda, enjoying every moment we had left with each other. We would go out of town on the weekends when I wasn't performing at a club. Sometimes we would open for big-name acts such as Luke from 2 Live Crew, Pastor Troy, Goodie Mobb, and many others. Many artists were from the Atlanta or Augusta areas, so if your music was professional and good, you had a better chance of getting on and being known throughout the city. As the time was approaching for me to head overseas, Miranda and I would have deep conversations about how we would proceed with our relationship. I discovered she had a daughter with her previous boyfriend, whom I never really saw or was around. This was shocking, but it didn't change the fact that I loved her. She went through some of my things while I was at work and found a "Promise Ring" that I had from Monique. We discussed that and the entire situation as I tried to explain Monique to her. She was confused about everything, and I felt the same way because things were starting to manifest and come to light. Why did all of this have to come out before I was preparing to leave? Although so much was coming to light, which could have easily ripped our relationship apart, we decided to stay together through it all and hoped it would work out.

The day had arrived when I was flying to South Korea and had orders to be placed in the 2nd Infantry Division at Camp Hovey. This location was not far from the DMZ; if something happened, Camp Casey and Camp Hovey were the main camps that were prepared to go to war first against North Korea. Miranda and I hugged and kissed each other for what felt like an eternity. As I boarded the plane, I had no clue what the future held for me. I was so used to things coming into my life and always leaving or being taken from me that I was somewhat numb to the feeling. It was a long, 19-hour flight to South Korea, and I was extremely happy to get off the airplane and onto hard ground with fresh air. The only thing is, once we landed, got our bags, and walked outside of the airport, the only smell that welcomed us was the human manure that the Koreans used to fertilize their rice fields. It was one of the worst smells I have ever smelled in my life!

CHAPTER 24

Welcome To Korea

ONCE WE ALL arrived at the airport, we loaded the buses and headed to the in-processing center in Yongsan. Yongsan is in Seoul, which is the capital of South Korea. This is where everyone wants to be stationed because they would have more freedom and many more activities. Seoul was also where all of the good clubs were located. As we entered the in-processing station, there were buses lined up on the outside along the street. Those buses were for the people that would be going up north to the 2nd Infantry Division. In the big gymnasium, we had our duffle bags next to us, and everyone sat on the floor. The administration person came out, introduced himself, and told us if we heard our name called, we should gather our bags and proceed outside to the buses. I was hoping I would not be going up north, but in the back of my head, I already knew it was coming. About 5 minutes into him calling out names, I heard "SPC Jason Mitchell." This was it. I grabbed my bags and proceeded to the bus. Once everyone was on the buses, we left. It was about a 2-hour drive to get to our next location, which was the "Turtle Farm" at Camp Casey. When you were new to the 2nd ID, they would call you a turtle. This is because so many new people would get drunk from the Soju and end up falling in the turtle ditches on the side of the road. People would be found knocked out or sleeping in these ditches. At the turtle farm, we were issued more gear because it was colder in this area of South Korea. We also filled out more in-processing paperwork and got our exact assignments. I was assigned to B Battery 2/17th Field Artillery unit at Camp Hovey. They told us that our units' representatives would pick us up in a few days after we were done in-processing all of our paperwork. I met a few guys at the turtle farm, and we decided to go to the "Ville." The Ville was a strip of clubs, bars, and shops right outside of the gate of Camp Casey. We went out and were offered some Korean drinks called "Soju." When you drink Soju, you have to mix it with juice or coke to make it easier to drink. We were warned about the Soju, but after drinking a few of them, we didn't feel anything. The only thing I remember after that night was waking up in my 4-man room with a couple of NCOs telling me that I thought the bathroom was in the middle of the floor. I urinated on the floor in the middle of the night and had no idea what was going on. They told me they tried to wake me up, but I was knocked out on my bed, almost like I was in a coma. This was why they would try to warn us about the Soju and tell us not to overdo it. I definitely found out the hard way.

The next day came, and our unit representatives picked us up. We drove about 20 minutes to Camp Hovey. There wasn't much going on in this camp, but luckily buses ran from Camp Hovey to Camp Casey all of the time. I arrived at my unit, and it was very strict. The first encounter I had was with a little skinny guy with glasses, who happened to be the 1SG. He asked who I was and began to curse me out. I was assigned a room with a KATUSA. KATUSAs are South Korean Army members fighting alongside the U.S. Army. They are required to serve a certain amount of time in the military, and most come from wealthier families. The ROCK soldiers are considered poorer and don't interact much with the U.S. Army. Therefore, they seemed to hate the KATUSAs. This unit was very different from the one at Fort Gordon. This was considered a Combat Arms unit. They had to be ready at all times for a war to break out, which meant that we trained consistently and always stayed in the field. For us to go to Seoul or anywhere when we weren't in the field, we would have to have a "Warrior Pass." This would allow us to go somewhere overnight and decompress and have fun. If we didn't have a Warrior Pass, we would have to be in our camps by 11 pm on the weekend and in our rooms by midnight. They would have people on duty that were called CQs. The CQs would do room checks by knocking on each door after midnight. They would open the door with the master key if you didn't answer. If you were not in your room, that was a huge mistake! You would receive extra duty, Article 15, a demotion in rank, and whatever else they wanted to do to you. This assignment was almost like a prison sentence. My NCO in charge of me was SSG Booker T. Johnson. He was tall, slim, bald with glasses, and he would work me like a slave. The KATUSA that worked with me would get over a lot of things. They were often drunk and too drunk to work. That means more work would fall on my lap. I didn't like it at all. To make time go by quicker, I tried out for the Korea Boxing Team at Camp Casey. This was actually an accident, as I was looking for the wrestling team. The coach told me that I should try it. I thought, "Why not?" and tried it out. I made the team, which relieved me from doing PT with my unit. I would have to go to Camp Casey to train with the boxing team for PT. I had never boxed before, but it was a great way to let out a lot of frustration and try something new. I was nervous, but I trained well and was ready for my first match. This was going to be the biggest match in Camp Casey as another guy who was one of the best boxers in South Korea and I were going to face off. This match was more spotlighted because I was representing 2/17 Field Artillery and he was from 1st Tank. The Army was similar to gangs during this time. Although we were fighting enemies as one force, we were against each other and very competitive when it came to other things. Tankers and Artillery soldiers could not stand each other. Everyone in my unit told me that if I lost, they would clown me for the rest of my time in Korea, which was a year tour! I don't think I ever trained so hard in my life. I couldn't let my unit down.

I was very nervous on the day of the fight because my whole unit was in one section of the gymnasium, and my opponent's unit was on the other side. They all had banners and were doing their chants. Everyone was wearing their unit shirts and hats. The atmosphere was crazy. As we both stepped into the ring to square off, I could see the nervousness in my opponent's eyes. The bell rang, and I went straight for him. I threw two punches, and he fell straight to the canvas. The referee began to count, "1, 2', 3, 4', 5." He got up and shook his head. All I could think to myself was, "I've got this guy now." We proceeded to box, and I caught him with a few good hits throughout the first round. As the bell sounded, we both went to our corners. My trainer was on the U.S. Army boxing team and told me I had this guy. He gave me some suggestions, and as soon as round two started, I went right for him again. We exchanged blows in the second round. He got me with a few good hits, and I got him with more hits. I stunned him again, and he received a standing seven count. The guys from my unit were screaming and acting crazy in the bleachers! I smiled at them and pointed as round two came to an end. The last and final round began, and I was trying to be smart to ensure I didn't get caught with a good hit and get knocked out. I boxed smart, not trying to knock him out but letting the clock run out as I knew I would win the match. Round three ended! I thought, "I made it through my first and probably most difficult match!" As we both went to the center of the ring, the scorecards were ready, and the referee raised my hand in victory, giving me my first boxing trophy! From then on, I was well respected throughout Camp Casey and Camp Hovey, including all of the guys in my unit. Nobody ever talked crap to me, especially the NCOs, who always looked out for me. A couple of guys in my unit thought they could beat me in boxing, so we laced up the gloves for fun. They only lasted about a minute before they tapped out. It was a funny sight to see. I competed in a few more matches across the peninsula and was undefeated in all my bouts. I got hit so hard that I broke a small bone in my wrist and didn't even know until I had to do a push-up. I couldn't put any pressure on my wrist. That was the last time I was able to box, but I enjoyed every minute of it while it lasted.

I would get free phone cards or special codes from some of the guys in my unit to call back to the States so I could talk to Miranda. When I first arrived, we would talk all the time, and I would receive cards 1-2 times a week. As time started passing, the cards started slowing down, and eventually, I wasn't even able to get in contact with Miranda. I didn't know what was happening but was told she was never home. Some of my friends would say they saw her in the clubs every now and then. Was our long-distance relationship too much to handle?

Were we done? As time passed, I began drinking more, going to clubs more, and partying more. I couldn't box with my broken wrist, so there wasn't anything else to do. I was only 21 years old. What else was I supposed to do? I hadn't heard from Miranda for almost 1-2 months, and when I was just about to count it as a loss, I got a letter and a phone call from her. We talked for hours and made plans for me to see her during my mid-tour. I loved her and didn't want to lose her again. I know the situation was hard for her, being a single parent and trying to make way for her and her daughter. I had no clue what she was going through, but I knew I wanted to spend the rest of my life with her. I saw the potential in her and the love she had in her heart for me as well. I thought long and hard and bought a wedding ring before it was time to return for my mid-tour vacation. I told SSG Johnson I was going to marry her. He didn't believe me, but I told him that I would do it and he would see me when I returned. I didn't have all of the answers or know how it was going to work, but I knew that we could figure it out together.

It was my 7th month in Korea, and the day finally came for me to take my mid-tour vacation. I boarded the plane with excitement to get to Augusta and see Miranda. The plane landed, and she picked me up at the airport. We hugged and kissed, and it felt right then that she was the one I was supposed to be with. Miranda got an apartment for her and her daughter, but it was in section 8, on the rough side of town. We were sitting in her apartment, and someone kept calling her, and a guy even pulled up outside of her apartment. I was so blinded by everything and too naive to believe anything she would tell me because I loved her so much. She told me the guy was just a friend and that I didn't have to worry about him coming back. The next incident happened when she was in the bedroom changing, and Shalite (her daughter) and I were in the living room talking. Shalita was young, but kids that young liked to talk. She told me that her mommy and a guy were in the room and they were making noises. I almost lost my mind! Miranda told me that she was just getting a massage and that Shalita was exaggerating. Once again, I was naive, but I was very angry! I took my bags and walked to the corner to meet the taxi cab. I was through with Miranda and was ready to get on the bus to head to Arizona to visit my friends before returning to Korea. She came to the corner crying and apologizing, telling me she didn't know what to do. She said I wasn't helping her with bills and didn't even know if she would ever see me again. In a way, I could see her point as we were both so young, partying and just trying to survive everyday life. I had no idea how hard it was for her to raise her daughter as a single mother in a rough part of town. Often, women think they need a man to help them or be there for them in these situations, and that's how many of these young women are raised to think. Miranda wanted better, but many circumstances kept her from thinking she could survive and do better without being another statistic. She was a kid raising a kid. As we both cried, laughed, slept, cried some more, and came to terms with the reality of our situation, I decided that I still wanted to marry her. I knew that if I married her, it would bring a sense of security to her life, and I could help take care of her. She wouldn't have to be in a section 8 apartment in the hood, and we could be a family. I only had a few more months left in Korea, and I would be coming back to the States.

I set up a date night, and we went to a nice restaurant in downtown Augusta.

They played live jazz music, and the atmosphere was very intimate. After about an hour, we finished our food and had a great time. This was it! I told her that I had something to ask her. I pulled out the ring and told her I wanted to be with her for the rest of my life. I asked Miranda if she would be my wife! I actually did it, and it just got real. She was so excited and replied, "Yes." We were both shocked and amazed at what had just happened. The waiter brought out the check, and when I looked at it, the price at the bottom reflected $145.00. I was only an SPC in the Army, and in 1998, $145.00 was a huge bill for dinner! We both looked at each other with our Bonnie and Clyde devious eyes and came up with a plan. I told her to go to the bathroom first and then walk out the back of the restaurant, which was close to the bathrooms. After I saw her go, I told her that I would do the same thing. We would meet about three blocks away, get a taxi, and head back to her apartment. The next thing I knew, we were both running down the road laughing hysterically and jumped into a taxi cab. We weren't even worried about any cops or someone coming after us. This was one of the best and most important nights of our lives! The next day, we called the courthouse and set an appointment to get married a couple of days later. We didn't tell anyone but her sister. When the day came for us to get married, we drove to North Augusta, where there was a nice gazebo with a beautiful background. At our marriage ceremony, it was just Miranda, her sister, and I. During the ceremony, we both had the giggles so badly that we could not stop. It was probably from being so nervous and not believing what we were actually doing, as we were really going through with our marriage. This was it, and it was now final. We were officially married on August 20, 1998. I flew back to Korea a few days later, and nobody could believe I had gotten married. They wanted me to go to the clubs and check out the girls, but that was the last thing on my mind. I was focused on doing the rest of my time and getting back to my new wife and now new daughter. I enrolled at the University of Maryland while I was in Korea. They had representatives in the camps in Korea with classrooms. I started going back to school and working out until it was time for me to leave. I received my orders about 60 days before, which stated that I would be going back to Fort Gordon. This was both a blessing and a curse at the same time. I had ties to all the people I was hanging around with who were nothing but trouble, and Miranda's family was there, which was a lot of dysfunction at the time. The blessing was that we would have help with Shalita, and we knew where the good parts of town were, so we could start right in our marriage by living together comfortably and getting on our feet as newlyweds.

CHAPTER 25
Newly Weds

THINGS WERE STARTING off good for us, being newlyweds. I flew back to Arizona to visit my family on the way back from South Korea and let everyone know about my new ventures. This was the first time I bought a vehicle on my own without any assistance, even with my bad credit from the repossession I had going into the military. I bought a Nissan Sentra and drove to Augusta, GA, from Tucson, AZ, only stopping once to sleep and, of course, gas stops. This was how excited I was to see my new wife. Once I arrived, we found a good apartment, we had a car, and everything seemed to be going well. I in-processed my new unit at the 67th Signal Brigade and was working as a Supply Specialist in A Co. 67th Signal Company.

Everything was going great, and I got another call from Miranda. She sounded very sad on the phone, and jokingly, I asked her if she was having twins. She asked me how I knew. I told her I was joking and to stop playing. She mentioned that the doctor told her she was pregnant with twins when she went for her checkup. Miranda fainted and fell to the floor. Once again, we were both devastated. I still liked partying and hanging out. We were newly married, but how could we handle three kids being so young ourselves? We contemplated having another abortion and drove to the facility. I heard something in my spirit tell me not to worry and that everything would be OK.

Something told me we did not have to go through with this. I told Miranda I loved her and was here for her. I let her know that we could handle this and that we didn't need to go through with another abortion. We were sitting outside the clinic when a lady came and handed us a brochure. I am unsure what the brochure had in it, but it was against abortion. We hugged each other, started the car, and left that place. We decided to keep our twins, not knowing what the future would hold for them or us.

Marriage was good at times but rough at other times. We would argue about various things, from simple to complex problems. We had no positive mentors in our lives, were not part of any church, and were continuously in chaos with

Miranda's family. There were times we were ready to give up and call it quits, but we decided to stick it out and stay together. The pregnancy didn't help due to hormone changes. This was one of the toughest seasons of life that we had to encounter. I was still recording music and hanging around the same crowds. I was still drinking and clubbing every chance I got. I was still young and wanted to enjoy life. The day came when it was almost time for the twins to be born. We were super nervous and rushed to the MCG hospital. They kept Miranda in the hospital room as it was nearing delivery time. Miranda began to feel pain, so the nurse entered the room and rushed her to the delivery room. I was very nervous and didn't know what I was supposed to do. This was my first experience with something like this, and I hated seeing my wife in pain. The delivery was going great for the first twin. However, the umbilical cord got caught and wrapped around the neck of the second twin. They had to go into an emergency C-section. Things were heating up, and I started to panic, thinking that one of the twins might not survive. An hour later, the nurse asked if I wanted to see my new daughters. When I walked into the room and saw them, I had a feeling I had never felt in my entire life. This was real, and these girls were my daughters! I never thought I would have kids, and now I have twins. It was exciting but very scary at the same time, not knowing what was to come. After admiring these beautiful princesses for an hour, the nurse had to take them to continue with whatever they did with them. They got the twins set up and monitored them to ensure they were OK. During this time, Miranda was asleep, and I hadn't eaten all day. I decided to walk across the street to Popeyes Chicken and grab something for dinner. I was so tired and standing at the counter trying to figure out what I wanted to order when the side door opened, and three guys walked in with stocking caps over their faces. I didn't even realize what was going on at the time that I said, "What's up to them?" They told me I knew what was up and to put my head on the counter. They put the gun on the back of my head while one of the other guys took money out of the register. He then asked me where my cell phone was. I told him that I didn't have one. He made me empty my pockets and didn't even take my cash. He made everyone in the restaurant go behind the counter and put us in the bathroom. One of the gunmen came back in and pointed the gun at all of us like he was ready to start shooting so there wouldn't be any witnesses. One of the other robbers called him, and he turned and went away. During this time, all I could think about was dying the same day my daughters were born into this world. I wasn't about to go out without a fight, so I opened the bathroom door and ran toward the back of the kitchen, where I kicked the door open. I didn't hear any gunshots and thought that was strange. As I turned around and looked back into the restaurant, I saw the robbers fleeing out the other side of the door. My heart was beating super fast, and my adrenaline was skyrocketing. At that point in time, it seemed like a light bulb had gone off in my head. Although I knew nothing about religion or Christianity for the most part, I knew that I had to stop living the way I was, or my daughters would grow up without a father in their life. It was at that point and time that I decided I was going to man up and be there for my girls no matter what happened.

I started to slow down on the fast life for the most part, but there were still times I would get that itch and want to explore with my friends. Now I had two precious daughters named Destiny and Alexxus that I was responsible for and needed to take care of. They came first, before any of our friends. Miranda's mother would watch the girls when we went out for the night or to give us a break. We were very grateful for those times; they helped us rekindle our marriage. My girls mean everything to me, and I would love to hold them and see them do all their first moments. One of the funniest moments I remember was putting some peach cobbler on the floor where I was sitting. I would put the girls on the other side of the room and watch them scoot to get to the peach cobbler. I would give them some, and it was like they turned into super babies! They would start doing flips on the floor and scooting all over the place. The girls could not be separated. Every time we put them on opposite ends of the bed, they would end up right back together. It was amazing to watch these girls grow. One day, I went to work, and my 1SG told me he had pulled an Ace card for me. I didn't know what he meant because I planned to leave the Army and go into Law Enforcement. He told me if I stayed, he would get me the location I promised to stay at, which was Ft. Sam Houston in San Antonio, TX. I couldn't believe he pulled it off, so I honored my word and re-enlisted on the spot. I called Miranda to tell her we would be PCS'ing to San Antonio within the next three months. She was shocked, happy, sad, and confused all at the same time. I didn't understand until we sat down and talked about what she had to tell me. During this time, we were having problems with Shalita acting out in school. Miranda's brother was sent to prison, and so much was going on at the time. Miranda told me that when she met with a social worker, the lady was a believer in Jesus and saw something in Miranda. She told Miranda that we would continue having problems in our marriage and our kids' lives if we didn't get away from Augusta. This was a day before I re-enlisted for Ft. Sam Houston. Miranda told me she spoke with her grandmother about us moving and had mixed feelings. At first, she was going to tell me to go, but her grandmother corrected her and told her that she needed to follow her husband, and everything was going to be OK. Miranda was sad but at peace knowing that her grandmother was the only one supporting our marriage by staying together and moving to Texas.

As the time came for us to pack and move to San Antonio, it was bitter-sweet. We created so many memories in Augusta. However, we needed to go and start our lives as our own family. We drove across the country with our family and three daughters. Once we got to San Antonio, we found an apartment called Oaks of Marymont, which seemed to be very nice and in a quiet area. I in-processed to my new unit, which was the Special Troops Battalion. I never saw anything like what I saw at this unit. The first thing that caught my attention as I entered the orderly room was a guy in an orange jumpsuit sitting on the sofa and shackled from his wrists to his ankles. I was very confused and wondered what I had gotten myself into. Come to find out, this guy was the Chaplain's Assistant and went AWOL and rented a car on a government credit card for two months. They thought they found him but instead arrested his twin brother. He eventually turned himself in so his brother wouldn't go to jail, and that is why I saw him sitting in the orderly room awaiting processing. Miranda seemed to enjoy San Antonio, but we still had some clubbing and drinking in our system. I always kept a six-pack of beer in the refrigerator, especially for Sunday football games. I began to like my job and transformed my company into a great supply and logistics unit. I was able to renovate three barracks and get the unit up to date on the computer system currently being used for supply transactions. I was now an NCO and was able to have soldiers under me as well as make decisions. It was a great transition, and I learned a lot over a few years. One day, I was at lunch and saw the guy I boxed in Korea for my first fight. He was medically discharged from the Army because a mortar caught one of his fingers and blew it off. He was from San Antonio and also played six-man league football. The six-man league was popular in San Antonio and some of the bigger cities. He told me I should play because he knew I used to play in high school. I told him I didn't know about that as I was a little older. He also gave me information about an actual semi-pro football league and told me they were about to start up, and one of the teams was looking for a QB. I told him that I would think about it. I went home, told Miranda about the idea, and asked her what she thought. We were going through another rough season in our marriage and life at the time. Away from her family, with three young kids, it seemed like Miranda was in a depressive state.

One thing that always kept me sane was writing and recording music. I continued making music and performing at a few places in San Antonio, but I wasn't feeling it as much as I used to. One night, I came back from the club to find the girls only had their diapers on, hadn't eaten dinner, the house was a mess, and Miranda was lounging around like nothing was wrong. I was furious, and we began arguing. I don't remember what she said, but whatever it was, it made me snap and grab her. I put her against the refrigerator and immediately came back to my senses. I thought, "What in the world was I doing?" She told me she was leaving and taking my girls. I don't recall all the details, but we ended up discussing everything that night, and she told me she needed to go back to church. I didn't understand it all and how the church would fix our situation. Besides, football came on during church services on Sunday, and I wasn't missing football. I ended up trying out for the starting QB position for a semi-pro football team called the San Antonio Aztecs. I didn't know how I would do it, but to my surprise, I ended up as their starting QB. This must have been the most thuggish team in the league, as most of our guys were coming out of jail, sniffing cocaine at the hotel after the games, smoking weed after practice, and so on. I was playing football now and working until about 2 or 3 pm every day because I had practice. My commander signed a waiver letting me play. Miranda started going to a church called Antioch Baptist Church on the east side of San Antonio and would always come home with a smile and a joyful spirit. I didn't understand it all. All she did was go to some boring church service where all the hypocrites were probably present and half the people were probably asleep during the service. She would always invite me and tell me I should come with her. I would thank her but refuse at the same time. I continued to go out with friends and have fun doing whatever I wanted. One day, it was raining, and a Yukon truck stopped in front of me. I hit my brakes but ended up skidding into the truck. The Yukon didn't have a scratch on it, but the front end of my car was smashed in. I could still drive it home, but it was really bad. This accident caused us to miss out on seeing the playoff game with the Lakers and Spurs. I also didn't know what I was going to do because we had three daughters, and now I didn't have a vehicle. I was going TDY to Ft. Hood for a class that Monday, and I had a rental vehicle. I didn't know if my plan would work, but I gave it a shot once I arrived and got my first break. I went to a dealership in Killeen, TX, and looked at a 2002 Ford Expedition. This vehicle was extremely nice, and its color was money-green. I did the test drive, came back, and inquired about the purchase. They ran my credit, put the numbers together, and I was in the truck that night! I didn't know how in the world I got that vehicle, but it was a miracle, especially with my credit at the time.

I returned to San Antonio, parked in the middle of the parking lot, decorated the inside with rose petals, and put on Avant's "Makin' Good Love" with all the doors open. I gave a note to a little kid playing to tell my wife to come to the parking lot. I had rims, a TV, and a new stereo system put in the Expedition, and it was shiny green. Miranda came out, started screaming, and took off running. I was laughing but confused. Why did she run? When I went to see what was going on, she had tears of joy and came back to the Expedition. She got in it, and we were so happy we could move forward without being crammed in a wrecked, smashed, small 4-door vehicle.

She asked me to come to church with her on Sunday. I thought about it, and just when she thought I was about to say no again, I surprised her with a "yes." She was excited. We got dressed and drove to Antioch Missionary Baptist Church with our girls. I didn't feel like going, but something was tugging at my heart and telling me to go. I enjoyed the breakfast before service and the lunch after service. I fell asleep during the service. There were times I would go and times I would miss. The main thing was that I wanted to play football. The current team I was on, the Aztecs, really sucked. I ended up playing for a more professional team with guys that were more serious about their careers. The team was called the San Antonio Rush. This team was good, and we missed the playoffs by 10 yards. I played very well for this team and drove them back into the game, including our loss and missing the playoffs. We had 30 seconds left in the game when I did a QB sneak from 10 yards out and scored a TD. We were up by 3 points with 30 seconds to go. The other team received the kickoff and ran it back to our 40-yard line with 15 seconds left. They threw a pass and got down to our 5-yard line with 8 seconds left. On the last play of the game, they ran an option left, and the running back took it in for the score and knocked us out of the playoffs. I played six-man football for the San Antonio Thunder after the season. Football was my life and kept me sane. However, it also kept me banged up pretty good. I had some cracked ribs and failed my PT Test because I couldn't do a sit-up. My 1SG understood because I always max out and go to the extended scale on my PT Test. Physical Training was never an issue for me.

Although we had our challenges and disagreements, we were beginning to be more at peace with each other. Our transition from Augusta took a lot for us to get used to. Miranda would always come home happy on Sundays with the girls in their pretty but country-looking dresses. We would always laugh and enjoy each other when she came home. I started to see her change and begin to walk in more of a mature role as a woman, mother, and wife. I saw this lady come to the house, checking on her and making sure that she had our girls fed, bathed, clothed, and in a clean home. This caught my attention because this was nothing we were used to seeing or having around us. Mrs. Levine was no joke and even started getting on me about coming to service. She would give me scriptures to read and ask me to explain them to her whenever she called or came over. It seemed like this lady cared about our family and us.

CHAPTER 26
My Transition

WHILE I WAS sitting at work on September 11, 2001, I heard some people calling everyone into the conference room where the TV was located. I didn't know how to react when I watched those planes crash into the twin towers. I knew it wasn't good. Being in the military, it was about to go down. Not even 20 minutes later, we got a call that we were on lockdown and to sign for our weapons as America was under attack. We had to get all our gear and begin putting it together as we waited for our next set of orders and the President of the United States' speech on what was going on. Ft. Sam Houston locked down the entire installation, and nobody could come on or off. This was not good. As the President gave his speech, we found out what happened. It was a terrorist attack. We were on high alert, and from this day forth, America, as we knew it, would never be the same.

On one particular Sunday morning, as Miranda was getting ready for church, I got out of bed and began to get ready. She was looking confused and asked where I was going so early. I told her I was going to church. She was shocked but excited at the same time. We both got the girls ready and headed to service. Something in my spirit told me that I needed to be at church on this day. I had no clue what it was, but it was a sense of urgency. As we pulled up to the church, I let Miranda and the girls out and went to park the truck. As I was walking up the sidewalk, I noticed a man looking at the building in confusion. As I got closer, with tears in his eyes, he turned toward me and asked, "What is this place?" I looked at him like he was crazy and told him it was a church. The man broke down even more and began to cry. I was confused and didn't know what to do. He started sharing how he lost his wife, daughter, job, home, and everything and had nothing else to live for. Right then and there, I started speaking biblical things to this man. It was like I wasn't even myself. I don't remember everything I told him, but I can vaguely remember it was scriptures within the Bible that I was breaking down to encourage this man. It was surreal, like Jesus Himself took over my body and started speaking through me to this man. I took this man to the church's elders and let them know he needed help. I explained what was happening to him, and they told me they would take care of him. I immediately went to the church service on the other side of the sidewalk in the main building and walked down the aisle straight to the front of the congregation where Pastor Walker was preaching. He asked if I needed to share something, and I said yes. I remember explaining what had happened outside and how the church needed to step up more, as so many people on the streets were hurting. At the time, I didn't know what I was doing or saying or knew anything about etiquette or protocol. I didn't care either. I wanted this church and its people to do something about all the hurting people I saw daily. I was tired of hypocrites. Once I sat down, the pastor preached a powerful message, and I told myself that I had lived for the world long enough. I said, "I give up." I will try to live for this God that these people talk about all the time. I had nothing to lose. I don't think things could have gotten much worse than they already were. During the altar call at the end of the service, I prayed the prayer, and I told Jesus that I would give everything up and live for Him from this day forward if He was real. I needed Him to show up in my life and show me He was real. I needed some kind of sign. I tried living by the standards of the world, and it almost got me killed numerous times. I made terrible decisions, went through unnecessary issues, and put my family through heartache. I had nothing to lose by trying something different and seeing if this Jesus these people were speaking of was really real or not. On that day in 2002, I surrendered myself and gave my life to Jesus Christ.

Soon after, I would be baptized and try to live out this Christian life everyone was speaking of. It was not easy in the beginning. However, we stopped drinking, watching pornography, and cursing within a short timeframe. It was like God recognized that we wanted to be delivered from those strongholds, and he recognized and honored that. Now we were facing another trial as Miranda was pregnant again. We didn't even think about abortion this time, but how we would care for yet another child. We pressed through and had another beautiful daughter named Alicia. From the first time I held her, I could tell she would be something special. She had a cute little birthmark on her nose and was a very happy baby. Miranda would always read the Bible to her while she was in her stomach and continue to play worship music to calm her down when she was born. Alicia had a special anointing in her life that time would eventually reveal later in life. With four daughters, we would continually face trials and challenges financially, but we continued to go to church and get around more people that were building us up and encouraging us to keep on pressing. I stopped rapping altogether, and music was no longer a part of my life. It seemed like everything was starting to fall into place. I was going back to school at St. Phillips Community College and attended Air Assault School, Airborne School, and Master Fitness Course. Life was becoming great and so much more fulfilling. When everything was beginning to get on track, we received orders for Ft. Lee, VA. How could this happen when everything was going so well and we had discovered a new family who was pouring into us? We had to leave yet again, but we didn't know anyone in Virginia this time. They told us it would be alright and not to worry about anything. They told us we were saved now and part of the kingdom family. They told us we are now His children, and He always watches over His children just as we do our own.

I got orders to attend Basic Non-commissioned Officers' Academy, which was an 8-week course at Ft. Lee, VA. I needed to attend this school in order to get promoted and move up in rank, especially to E-7/Sergeant First Class. I didn't like the feeling of leaving Miranda with all of the girls, but I had peace about it, knowing that our church family promised us they would assist and help her out with anything she needed. That brought me a lot of comfort, knowing she was in good hands. I still didn't like that I would be without her and my girls for that long period, but being in the military, it was bound to happen, especially as you increase in rank. As I left for school, we were still trying to figure out how our PCS would work, as she was in San Antonio, and I was in Virginia, where we would already be stationed. We had to do a lot of coordination over the phone and ensure that everything was being packed, the apartment cleaned, utilities closed out, etc. It was hectic and awkward, but we were able to make it happen. While I was in school, the classes were long during the days and stressful as we had guard duty for just about everything due to the 9/11 situation. When we were free on the weekends, the only thing we wanted to do was relax and have some fun. As a class, we would go out to dinner or to Richmond to some clubs or fun places to help our time go by. I struggled with going to some of these locations because I didn't want to go back to my old self of drinking and partying like I used to. Now I made a commitment and dedication to Christ to try to walk this life as He would want me to as much as possible. It was hard. Sometimes I won. Sometimes I lost the battle, but I never quit or gave up. Our class was almost over, and we were on our last weekend. We had planned for weeks that our class would go out together for our last weekend and have fun celebrating the end of our BNCOC Academy. To my surprise, my wife and the girls showed up the same weekend. They didn't tell me they were coming, but they just showed up in the parking lot. I was mad and frustrated but happy to see them. I didn't understand why she would drive all the way and not let me know anything. What if something had happened? I didn't plan for a place for them to stay or anything. I had to jump through hoops trying to get all of this done, and I was going to miss our class event as well because of this. We got into a huge argument, and I told her I would be at the NCO Club celebrating with my class, and afterward, I would be back, and we could figure everything out. I went to the NCO Club and hung out with everyone, and one of the females in my class was standing by me at that particular time and was talking to me. My wife was spying throughout the night and decided to come over and cause a scene, telling me I needed to come outside now. It was embarrassing at that moment because she had a plain white T-shirt on, her hair was not combed, and she was not dressed up. We were both still young and had different thoughts on a variety of things. We didn't know anyone at Ft. Lee. Otherwise, my thoughts were to have a sitter watch the girls and have her come with me. Just showing up out of nowhere definitely didn't help those circumstances. When we were outside, we argued about the entire situation. She thought the girl standing by me wanted me. Nothing I could say would ease her mind as it was already made up. I felt like giving up and not even trying to explain anything. After a long, long, long conversation, we both calmed down and were able to work through the situation. It was partially my fault because she had some trust issues dealing with my ex-girlfriend. I also felt like it was partially her fault for having trust issues because of what she had done in the past while I was in Korea. When you combined these two, it didn't make the situation any easier.

I was assigned as an instructor for the Unit Supply Sergeant Basic Non-commissioned Officers Academy. This was the same place where I had just graduated from school; now I was going back to be an actual instructor. Everyone knew what happened at the NCO Academy, and I was embarrassed to return here. They wanted me as an instructor because I was at the top of my class and was in Fitness Group 1, which many instructors could not keep up with. I had all the traits, skills, and abilities to be one of their best instructors, so they pulled me in. As an instructor, I enjoyed meeting many soldiers in the same MOS (job) as I was. In the field I was in, you didn't see many of us as there were only 1-2 in every company, if that many. So to see 20–30 people in a classroom at one time was amazing. I met a lot of great soldiers and was able to share my knowledge and wisdom with many of them. Some were coming back from the war in Iraq and shared many of their stories and wisdom with the class, and others were preparing to depart once they returned to their duty station. There were so many things that happened that opened my eyes as an instructor at BNCOC. We had a student that was sleeping around with different girls and ended up sleeping with a married woman. The worst part is that this guy was HIV positive, and the married woman had a husband and kids. She ended up on suicide watch, and the soldier was sentenced and went to prison. Another incident had a soldier collapse after a unit run and die on the spot as his heart stopped. It seemed like a black cloud was over this place. I couldn't go to church every weekend like I wanted because I had to be at formation on Sundays with my class I was instructing for accountability. I felt like I was getting more distant from God. Just when I felt this fading feeling, Miranda asked me if I wanted to attend a couples' marriage group bible study in our neighborhood on post. I was all for it as it was after I got off work and once a week. We would gather and discuss the bible and marriage's good, bad, and ugly moments. The couples were awesome, and we were able to form a bond and stay accountable to each other. Derrick asked if I wanted to attend a Men's Conference in Atlanta at Creflo Dollar's church. I had no clue who he was, but Derrick paid for me to go, so I accepted the invite.

This would be a life-changing moment for my family and me. We were still having problems with Shalita acting out in school, and I needed all the parenting, manhood, husband, and fathering skills I could get. When we were there, the conference had about five guest speakers who spoke on various topics. One key aspect that helped change me was budgeting and putting things in place. I took so many notes at this conference that I filled up an entire yellow legal pad of paper. When I returned home, I sat Miranda down and told her what we would do. There was no longer "my account" or "her account." It was going to be "our account." We were going to put things in place to help us better budget and account for our money, so we weren't living paycheck to paycheck. We were going to do things differently from this point forward. She told me she didn't know who I was when I returned from that conference. She was so happy and excited that her prayers were being answered. I still wasn't making any music at this point, and Miranda gave me a Christian Hip Hop CD that she had bought. I took out Kanye West's "College Dropout" CD and put it in the CD player. The music was so corny and ridiculous that I took it out and tossed it down the highway as we were driving. The blessing side to that is that at the Men's Conference, I found a Christian Rap compilation album that had a guy named Canton Jones on it. I had never heard of this guy, but he was on most of the tracks, and I had never heard Christian music, especially rap that was glorifying God! I didn't think you could even do anything like that. Was this right? I played this CD every day until I came across another album by another Christian rapper named Lecrae. Suddenly, I was finding more and more Christian Rap music I could relate to that wasn't corny and sounded really good. There were many more artists, including Mr. Del, C-Micah, K-Drama, D-Maub, Ziklag Boys, and many others. Then I found a website that was dedicated to Christian Rap music called DaSouth.com. This was where all the artists would come together to chat with the fans, and it seemed like a big happy family.

Now I had a marriage group I was attending, music I could listen to that was edifying me, and everything was going well once again. I decided to put in a Warrant Officer packet to see if I would be selected. I had always heard of Warrant Officers and knew they were the technical experts in their fields, but could I become one? It was very hard to get selected as you had to put together a long packet with many attachments and recommendation letters. Once I put my packet in, it was a waiting game until the next board to see if I was selected for my MOS. After a couple of months, the results came back, and I wasn't selected. I wasn't frustrated, but now I was at my $7^{1}/_{2}$yr mark in the Army, and if I wasn't going to be an officer, it was time to go. I was starting to look at the FBI and U.S. Marshals for my next career. The only thing is, once your Warrant Officer packet is a Non-Select, it automatically goes before the board for a second look. About two months later, during one of my classes, one of my students told me that he had the list for the E-7 board results, and I was on it. Another student was at my computer looking up the Warrant Officer results to see if he made it, and he called me into the office to tell me that I was on the list this time! This was crazy. I served in the Army for $7^{1}/_{2}$ years and was placed on the E-7 and Warrant Officer lists at the same time. Now I had a big decision to make. I told Miranda, and we wrote out all of the pros and cons for each decision we could make and ended up in favor of going the Warrant Officer route. About four months later, I had a class date and headed to the Warrant Officer Candidate Course in Ft. Rucker, Alabama. I had heard horror stories about Warrant Officer school, and now I was about to find out for myself.

CHAPTER 27

New Seasons

DAY 0 OF the Warrant Officer Candidate Course took me back to the first day of Basic Training. I began to second-guess my decision to enroll in this course. The instructors were barking commands in our faces. We were carrying all of our gear around the entire building to get to a point about 30 yards away. Once we got into the building, we had to do wall squats, push-ups, flutter kicks, and duck walks while sounding off with various commands they would give us. This continued for about 2 hours. We were told to get in our beds and had 10 minutes to unpack, make our beds, and get in our PT clothes under the covers with our lights out. This was ridiculous! As soon as my eyes closed, it seemed like this nightmare was starting again. We had to be downstairs in formation within 7 minutes of them turning the hallway lights on and hearing them say, "Good morning, Candidates." Not only did we have to be downstairs and in formation, we also had to ensure our beds were made properly, we were in the right uniform, and our teeth were brushed. As we walked at a high-speed rate (we could not run) past each instructor, we had to stop and give them the greeting of the day. The greeting of the day consisted of your name, a proper greeting, the word of the day, and your name again. You could not go on until they acknowledged you. It would sound like, "Sir, Candidate Mitchell, Good morning, Integrity, Candidate Mitchell." They would acknowledge it by saying, "Continue, Candidate." It was something I had never seen before, and being in the military for seven years, I already knew what to expect in your units. This training was designed to re-break you and throw you a curveball. We could not have any caffeine until we earned caffeine rights. Every second of the day was planned with a schedule. When we ate, there was a certain format, and our silverware had to be placed on the table in a certain way. We had to eat like robots, which consisted of our heads straight and eyes forward, arms and shoulders squared, bringing the food to our mouths one time, arms down, silverware down, chewing, picking up our napkin, dabbing our lips, napkin down, one drink of your beverage, beverage down, and repeat. It was ridiculous! We were the last official class that had to do what they called "Dining Rights." During the day, we would be in classes all day and have to score at least 80% on each test or we would fail the course. You would get one retake, but you only had so many retakes for the entire course. If you used up your three retakes in the beginning and failed a test towards the end of the course, you would fail the course because you were not allowed to do another retest. This course was intense, but as the weeks passed, we were given more privileges, which helped us get through the days. As a former instructor, a few people in my class knew me, which interested the TAC Officers. They asked me how everyone knew who I was, and I could not lie because that was an integrity violation, which automatically gets you kicked out of the course. I told them I was an instructor. I was in great shape, so every time they tried to "smoke" me, it didn't bother me much, and I would smile a lot. This got me the nickname "Smiley Bird" with all of the TAC Officers. Since I was an instructor, they wanted to prove a point to me, and the rest of the candidates that they didn't care and I wouldn't get any special treatment.

During the course, we were given WOC guides, which everyone referred to as Warrant Officer School Bibles. It was designed so that you could not win because everyone interpreted the information in it differently. It would have specific instructions on how to set up your drawers for display; roll your socks; fold your t-shirts; underwear; place your clothes on the hanger and rack inside your wall locker; etc. Since our dressers, bunks, and wall lockers all faced different directions, we all had different perceptions of how our display would be set up. In the middle of the night, you would hear TAC Officers walking down the hallway and tapping candidates in their bunks, telling them to get their stuff and go back to HHC. HHC was the holding company where you would wait to start everything over again from the beginning. I remember being four days away from graduation and hearing the TAC Officers walking down the hallway. I prayed hard that they would not stop by our room. There were five people they sent back to day 0 to wait for the next class to begin the whole thing all over again. The only way to fail the course is to fail your tests, commit integrity violations, or quit. Their goal was to make as many people quit as possible. The day came when we were being presented with our awards, the day before graduation. If you made it this far, you were graduating unless you did something extremely stupid the day before graduation. I received the Physical Fitness Award, which means that only two people in your class will receive this award for having the highest PT Score in their class. I was proud, but more than that, I was eager to get off Ft. Rucker as soon as possible. I lost so much weight in this school that my wife drove right past me and didn't even recognize me! After the graduation ceremony, I quickly put my stuff in the truck and told my wife, "Let's go before they change their minds." It's funny now, but at the time, it wasn't funny at all. It was worse than being in a prison.

The next phase would be the Warrant Officer Basic Course. This was the course that each candidate had to go through to learn and be a subject matter expert in their chosen field. My MOS was a 920A Property Accounting Technician. This meant I controlled all of the Army's equipment for whatever Brigade I was assigned. I would ensure that every unit had all the equipment needed or ordered everything they were short of. I would ensure all equipment was accounted for and signed by the company commanders and report any missing, lost, damaged, or destroyed equipment or property. It was a big task, especially if you were being assigned to a brigade, which meant that you would have 36 companies that you would be responsible for tracking thousands of pieces of equipment. It was a lot of responsibility, but I was ready to learn more and take on this task. The hard part was over, and now in the Basic Course, the instructors tried to get us to calm down and relax. They told us that we were no longer in the Candidate Course and were now officially considered Warrant Officers. That eased everyone's minds and made the course more enjoyable. The Basic Course was much different, and we didn't have anything to worry about as long as we passed our tests. Another thing that made the course more bearable for me was that I was already stationed at Ft. Lee, so I could go home and sleep in my bed every night. I was able to see my wife and girls every night.

It felt like I was going to school during the day and coming home in the evening. Once the Basic Course was a few weeks away from completion, we received our assignments. My next assignment would be Ft. Carson, Colorado, with the 2nd Infantry Division. This was the only unit to ever deploy from Korea to another war zone, Iraq, and then to Ft. Carson. It would be a few months before I would head out to Ft. Carson, so I was assigned back to the NCO Academy for accountability until I PCS'd. I didn't have a job at the time, so I had more time to listen to more music from some of the new Christian artists I was coming across. As I was sitting at the computer desk one day, it hit me. I asked my wife if she thought I could do the same thing these guys were doing: make Christian Rap music and bring people closer to God with music that edifies rather than the music I was making before, which was leading them far from Him. She told me to pray about it and see. I did and got an extreme peace about it. I found a site that sold instrumentals and began writing my first few songs. The first song I ever wrote and recorded was "He Saved Me." I didn't want my music to be corny like the CD my wife gave me, so I bought a great instrumental and ensured I had a rugged, grimy flow that was popular at the time, similar to Master P. I was writing and driving to Richmond to record at a professional studio while preparing to move. It was like I had a huge hunger to get my first EP done and handed out to as many people as possible. My EP was completed about two weeks before we were ready to leave for Colorado. I was excited and nervous at the same time. I thought, "Were people really going to accept this and play it?" I started handing the music out to everyone I could, and the next thing I knew, I would hear people driving by on the roads in Ft. Lee playing my music. This was amazing. I had the secular concept of the music business down but didn't know much about the Christian music industry. All I knew was that I wanted to create music that would uplift people and provide them with something they could play and listen to in their vehicles without feeling embarrassed when their friends rode with them. That was my goal, and it seemed to work. I started connecting with more people on MySpace and DaSouth.com. I didn't know anyone in Colorado, but I was excited to meet more people there that were doing the same thing.

As we began our transition to Colorado, our main focus was finding a good, solid church and a nice home. I was now a Warrant Officer and getting paid much more than I was when I was an E-6. Our girls were growing so fast, and the decision to become a Warrant Officer seemed to be a great one. Once I arrived at my unit, my thoughts on the whole thing slowly changed. This was one of the worst units I have ever seen or heard of. Unfortunately, these guys were gone from their families for two years because they were in Korea for a year and then came on orders to deploy to the war in Iraq for another year. Their main location was Ramadi, Iraq, which was one of the worst places to be in the country at the time. Over 80% of the Brigade were divorced, and some of the soldiers, including high-ranking officers, ended up marrying or sleeping around with each other. It was so bad at this time that lower enlisted soldiers were running meth labs out of the barracks and prostitution rings. I have never seen or heard of anything like this before. As I transitioned to this unit, they were also going through many changes, including turning from a Heavy Brigade to a Light Brigade. This meant that they would be downsizing. As a Property Accounting Technician, this was a huge responsibility for me as I had to turn in thousands of pieces of equipment or transfer them to other Army units across the United States that were preparing to go into combat. On top of this, I was a brand new Warrant Officer, and the Brigade was transitioning to a different logistics accountability system. I was blessed to have the NCO with the Brigade through the transition of two years to be there with me. He was my continuity, and I leaned on him very heavily for anything I didn't know or understand at the time. I learned so much during my time with this Brigade. These guys were mentally drained, ill, and needed a break, but they came back on orders to deploy to Iraq again. There was no way that I would go with this Brigade to Iraq in the condition it was in. As this was going on, Miranda found out she was pregnant again! How in the world could this be happening again, and now I was on deployment orders for Iraq? I couldn't leave my wife with all these kids, at least not at this point. She was pregnant with our fourth daughter and fifth daughter altogether. I would be crazy to leave her, and she would probably break down during her pregnancy. All of this was happening at the same time we were plugged into a great church called CFAN (Church For All Nations), and my music was starting to take off even more.

Somebody at my church told me to get a hold of this guy named JayMay once he returned from Iraq. They said he was in the military but owned his own independent record label. I was curious and interested in meeting this guy, especially at the same church I was a part of. A few weeks passed, and JayMay was at the Sunday service. We met and set a date to discuss what we could do together. I was excited to meet such a humble, down-to-earth brother willing to help me on this journey. I told Miranda about him, and she seemed excited for me. She was still going through her battles of knowing I was on deployment orders and her pregnancy with yet another girl. There had to be a way for me not to have to deploy. It wasn't that I didn't want to fight or go to Iraq, but the timing was horrible. I found out that I qualified as a sole survivor due to being the only surviving son of my mother. I had a step-brother, but that didn't count as we were not full brothers. This was my ticket to not having to deploy at this moment so I could stay home and take care of my wife and family and pursue the Christian music ministry. Once JayMay and I linked up more, I signed with his independent label, Double Edge Sword Records. Everything was beginning to run smoothly again. I was plugged in and serving at church; music was taking off; I was with my family, and now I was a part of a label. I would tell all of my soldiers that came into the office, and they would ask me for a CD. I gave them CDs and posters, and one particular soldier stood out. He went by the name "Da Clay." I didn't know he rapped as well, but he told me he liked what I was doing, which influenced him to start making more Christian Rap music. Eventually, we all linked up, and I introduced Da Clay to JayMay. Da Clay ended up signing with Double Edge Sword Records as well. We were beginning to have a strong roster and were making an impact in Colorado Springs. Other people were doing smaller venues in the city, but once we got going, we began doing some powerful work across Colorado Springs and Denver. Miranda was doing her Women's Bible Study group at the house, and I connected with many men and artists around the country. We opened for a particular event for Canton Jones, the same guy I heard at the beginning of my journey on this Christian walk. It was amazing. I ended up moving to the 1st Army Division West, which gave me more time to work on my music. I didn't have to deploy, and now I was at home doing shows and concerts across Colorado and starting to expand to other states, such as Texas and Oklahoma. This was the same time I made my first real album, "Tha Arrival." I still remember taking the picture that was on the front cover in my basement. There were a few songs on Tha Arrival that took off on DaSouth.com and MySpace, as well as through some major Christian networks. The songs were called "Take It To The Church Floor," "Okay," and "They Don't Know." It was definitely different from what traditional church folks were used to hearing. It was a mix of Lil John and Master P in a Christian version, providing a relevant and real message that edified people that were not church people. It was exciting to see my song included on a compilation that was nominated for a Stellar Award, the world's second largest Christian awards show. I thought it was fun doing shows in different cities and seeing people dance to the Christian Rap music that I created.

One night, I was asleep and woke up in a cold sweat. Miranda asked me what was wrong, and I told her that I thought Satan was messing with me in my dreams. I told her he wanted me to go to a downtown park called Acacia Park, where all the homeless people were always located. He wanted me to wash their feet and pray with them. She laughed and told me it wasn't Satan but the Lord trying to strip my pride from me. I immediately got up in the morning and loaded a bunch of clothes, a cooler with hot water, and my gloves into the truck. Miranda told me to hold on until she got dressed because she wanted to see this for herself. We headed to Acacia Park, and there were always many homeless people in this park every day. On this day, there were no homeless people to be seen anywhere! I felt a little relieved, and as we were preparing to leave, down one street, about ten homeless people were standing in the street. I told the Lord that I was ready and to use me however He could. When I pulled up and parked, I walked over to them, nervous, shaking, and unsure how they would react to my request. I walked up to them and told them they might think I was crazy, but the Lord told me to wash their feet. They looked puzzled but told me it was OK, and they didn't need their feet washed. I was relieved and told them I also had clothes for them. They were interested in the clothes, and all came by the truck and took what they needed. As I began talking to them and gave them a message that I felt God was leading me to give them, a couple of them began to tear up. I asked them if they had ever given their life to Christ, and they told me they never had. I asked them if they wanted to pray and receive Christ into their lives, and they said they did. That day, about five of the homeless guys gave their lives to Christ and thanked me for sharing that opportunity with them. This was the first time I ever stepped that far out of my comfort zone, but it was also very fulfilling and rewarding. This was better than any concert or show I had ever performed at. After I was obedient to what God was telling me to do, it was like so many doors were beginning to open all over the place. I was getting booked for shows across the United States, and they gave me honorariums. I wasn't used to honorariums because I would drive to different states on my own dime to perform a 10-minute set. Sometimes I would drive from Colorado Springs to Houston, TX, or Oklahoma City for a 5–10 minute set. People thought I was crazy at that time, but in the same way, they thought I was crazy. I still have some of my best friends and connections from those moments in 2006-2007 to this day in 2018. It was a very interesting time and very frustrating at the same time. The same way Jesus wasn't welcomed in His own home is the same way JayMay and I felt about our church. They were booking us all across the country, but we never performed or shared our gifts at our own church for the congregation or the youth group. The youth pastor was into a heavy rock music feel, and it hurt to see so many urban students standing outside the youth group room during the praise and worship session. We tried to mix it up and bring a different vibe, but we were always turned down. This created a hardened heart towards the youth pastor and the church because we wanted to see everyone being able to praise Jesus, not just the hardcore rock Christians. I didn't want to go to this church anymore, but Miranda was plugged into the Women's ministry and was also serving. The messages were always about politics or business-centered, and it seemed like the Gospel was missing. I felt like I wasn't being fed anymore, but I wanted to keep my family happy as this was where they connected well with many people. We made many connections in Colorado Springs and Denver with so many people. This is one of the places I considered as a second home. During my album release party, we wanted to throw one of the biggest Christian music events to hit the city. We invited Lecrae as the special guest artist and had many other artists as guests during the event.

The event was called the MidWest Music Fest and was a huge success. We had over 1,500 people at this event, and hundreds of people gave their lives to Jesus during the altar call. We saw drug dealers, gang members, and people who had no idea what was going on in their lives turn to Jesus. It was one of the most beautiful sites I had ever seen. This was the moment that I realized that this music ministry was more than fun; it was life-changing and nothing to play with. From this day forth, that is how I looked at the Christian rap ministry. I made mistakes along the way that I learned and grew from, especially being married and being an artist. Whether you're a secular or Christian artist, you will have girls flirting with you or coming at you with wrong motives or intentions. As I was so focused on bringing the music to everyone, I was blinded by some of the schemes of the enemy at the time that almost tore apart my marriage. I didn't realize that it was wrong for two guys to go with two women we weren't married to on a booking to Florida. In our eyes, it was very innocent as one of them was our booking and management person. I didn't think to ask myself why everyone asked if these ladies were our wives, and when we told them no, how people were looking a little confused. It was nothing to us, but the perception was not very good. Unfortunately, we didn't have mentors telling us that decisions like that were stupid and would cause hardships in our marriages. Even though we were on different sides of the hotels and everything was innocent on both sides between them and us, the whole perception and concept of traveling with women that were not our wives wasn't very wise at all. This was a hard lesson to learn and caused my wife to have more trust issues and bitterness within her heart toward me. Although I couldn't understand it at the time, I was blinded by all the lights, fame, and fans shadowing me with love. I felt like my wife didn't want me to succeed or make the music anymore, which caused me to have a hardened heart toward her. During this time, our last daughter, Jasmine, was born. She was another one that was very special, and you could tell that she was going to be a force to reckon with when she got older. As I held her in my arms, all I could think of was her being born in the same place I was born in, Colorado Springs at Fort Carson. Again, I told myself that I would always be here for this little girl, and I was looking forward to making a bright future for her.

CHAPTER 28

Korea Part II

ALTHOUGH THINGS WERE going great in Colorado Springs, and we made many friends through our outreach and concert events, I received orders to head back overseas to South Korea for a second tour. I couldn't believe I had to leave my family again, especially after everything had gone so well. I discussed the transition with Miranda, and although I didn't want to go, I had to. We decided to go back to San Antonio, where she would have strong support in place from our Antioch Church family. We packed up and headed back to San Antonio with our girls. I found a three-bedroom apartment on the outskirts of a great area with good schools for our girls to attend while I was gone. Once we moved into the apartment and got everything set up, the time was closing in on having to head out. My main focus was ensuring my family was well taken care of as I was on the other side of the world.

It was time to leave, and we headed to the airport with all of my luggage. Once again, this military life was taking a toll on me. I was very upset about leaving my family behind, but this is what we all signed up for, and I had to pay the bills for the family. If I didn't work, we didn't eat. We all hugged, and I kissed my girls and wife goodbye. I told them I would see them very soon, within 5-6 months. I had to stay strong for them and keep them encouraged during this season. We had most of the bills set up on direct deposit, alleviating my wife's many headaches. She didn't have to figure out what needed to be paid and could concentrate on being there for our girls during this season. Once I got to Korea, it was much different than the first time I arrived. Now I am an officer. I was sent to Camp Casey to be the Property Book Officer for the Fire Brigade. I was treated with a lot more respect and freedom. My barracks room had a bedroom, full bathroom, kitchen, and living room. It was almost similar to a small apartment. This tour was going to be much better than my last tour.

I figured out my job and made sure everything was going well, and after I had everything under control, I started to get back to my music. I was working out every day, writing and recording in my studio. I found a bible study to be a part of. It was right outside the gate and had everything I needed. I was able to focus on working on my next album, which was called Kingdom Music. I was meeting people in my bible study group and church services who were exposed to Lecrae and a few others, but not much Christian Hip Hop music. I wanted to be the change for them and let them see that there were more of us artists out here doing it and reaching people for Christ. I emailed many clubs to see if I could perform at their spots. One particular club emailed back. It was called Club Circle in Seoul. This was one of the biggest clubs in Seoul, and popular artists, such as Usher, Ne-Yo, Ying Yang Twins, etc., performed in this location. The club's co-owner invited me for an audition to see if they would have me perform a concert. I was nervous, but at the same time, I knew this was what I was supposed to be doing while I was in Korea. I was across the other side of the world, reaching people for Jesus Christ. Once I auditioned, the owner liked me and my music and asked if I wanted to perform the following month. Of course, I told him I would. They promoted the event on Korean television, and I saw flyers all over downtown Seoul with my picture on them. This was going to be an amazing event. While I was preparing and getting ready for the event, I met some other brothers that were making Christian Rap music. They were named the Bloodshed Beats and were on fire for the Lord. It was like God surrounded me with other like-minded believers to show me I wasn't alone. I also met another guy named Trinity, who I would hang out with, and we encouraged each other. Trinity was the one who first introduced me to off-post bible studies. Everything was lining up very well. I was invited to perform at some other church events across Korea, as well as some other military posts. I did a photoshoot at one of the biggest hotels in Seoul for my promo pictures and filmed one of my first videos to a song from Kingdom Music titled "Rescue Me." I was focused and was doing what God had called me to do in another country. It was amazing! The day came when it was time to perform at the club in Seoul, and I was super nervous, but I had my brothers with me. I had a backpack full of CDs to give away for free, and we were treated like royalty. The co-owner took us to our private room with fruit platter trays and meat for everyone. After about 30 minutes, the security guards came in and asked me if I was ready to go on. I told him, "Sure." I had Bloodshed Beats with me for my hype men, and we were ready to turn up in Club Circle. The security guard escorted me around to the garage to an elevator. When I looked up, 5 Lambos and a couple of Porsches were parked on this floor. I was confused about where we were going and started getting nervous. We entered another elevator, and the security guard handed me a cordless mic. The elevator stopped, and he told me, "Good luck," as we walked off onto some kind of platform. The guy that was by the platform told me I could start talking on the mic, and my music had just started. I was super confused now because I had no clue where I was. The next thing I know, he pushes a button, and the platform starts lowering. I could hear people screaming, and soon I started seeing the people as the platform lowered from the club's ceiling into the stage. There was a full wall with my picture on it, and the DJ was getting the crowd hyped as I came down. This was amazing, and we were definitely ready now! The club was packed, and the entire show went very well. All the people were hyped and seemed to love the music as they danced all night. I was able to share the message of Jesus through my music, and after our set, I was able to mingle and talk with some of the people. I gave away about 50 CDs at this event and prayed that the CDs would sow a seed in the lives of everyone that had one. This was one event I will never forget as long as I live.

After the event, I met one of the first Korean rappers to start Hip Hop in Korea. I didn't believe him because I didn't think there were Korean rappers. His name was Tiger JK, and he was a member of a group that was so popular in Korea that they referred to him as their Tupac. Skeptical as I was, we would hang out on the weekends more often, and it seemed like everywhere we went, people were in shock. He would get free clothes in every clothing store we walked into; free food in every restaurant we ate; he was well respected. When I got back on base, I asked the KATUSA that worked for me if they knew him, and they said, "Of course, he is very famous." They asked me how I heard of Tiger JK, and I told them, but they didn't believe me. Luckily, this was a good friend now, so I had his cell phone number and called him. I told him what was going on and handed the phone to the KATUSA, and the KATUSA fainted on the floor. This was very weird but funny. After that day, it seemed like all the KATUSAs would come to my office every day and all the time. God was really up to something and was setting so many things in place. I was able to put on the first Christian Hip Hop event called Kingdom Music Fest at Camp Casey. We had different musical and poetry artists share their gifts. This was the first time they ever had a Christian music event like this at Camp Casey, and everyone really enjoyed it and had a great time. As I became more and more known throughout South Korea through my music, some people would come along and try to take advantage of my gift or girls trying to flirt. I was so focused that I didn't realize it or was blinded, but I was able to stay focused throughout my entire tour. Even some of the military officer women were trying to be sneaky and flirt with me on the low, but I never really paid them any attention. My goal and focus were to get my new CD out and to create more shows. In the back of my mind, I thought to myself, what would I look like messing with these women? But I am out here spreading the message of Jesus through my music. I believe God protected me and brought that conviction to my spirit to keep me grounded and on the right path. I had many brothers and sisters in the faith that kept me in prayer and grounded as well, which helped tremendously. God was using me to deliver His message to these people, but at the same time, he was stripping me of pride in my heart so that He could use me even more for His kingdom. This was an exciting tour. I was so focused on Korea that I lost a little focus on my wife, as the enemy used that to slide in. I should have known something was off and not right when I came home on leave. It seemed like the atmosphere was off; people working at the apartment complex looked at me like they wanted to say something, but it was none of their business. Miranda was very hesitant and jumpy when I was using the computer at the apartment clubhouse. The maintenance guys always seemed to have a smirk on their faces, but I was again blind to anything that was happening. After I left to return to Korea a few months later, I flew back to Ft. Lee for the Advanced Course. This is where everything started to come out. I am not the type to snoop around, but something told me to go into her email. I did and found information about her and a married guy that lived on the same floor at the apartment complex she was staying in. The guy would take her trash to the dumpster and be outside washing his car with his shirt off. He would always confide in Miranda about his relationship and his sex addictions. The last email I read was a furious one from my wife asking him if he just enjoyed the act because he wasn't responding to her and was trying to stop their emails or relationship. When I read that, I was furious and ready to kill someone. This took all of my Christianity out of me as I got all the alcohol I could get my hands on and began drinking again. I sent him an email telling him everything I would do to him when I found him, but with no response. That made me even more upset, so I contacted his wife, who was an LTC in the Army. She told me that he has always been that way, and that's just how he is. It was like she was used to him cheating on her and always messing around. She seemed numb to everything and like she didn't care. Since I wasn't getting anywhere, I drank even more. I couldn't hold it in anymore, so I called Miranda and cursed her out. She couldn't understand what I was so upset about. I told her that I didn't want to be with her anymore and to never contact me again. I told her she could have everything but to leave me alone. She didn't want to give up on our marriage, so she hopped on the next plane to Richmond. I was cordial and headed to the airport, picked her up, and picked up another 12-pack of Corona. When we went to my hotel room, she explained everything that was happening and what had happened. She told me that I left cracks open and she was vulnerable, but nothing happened. She told me he knocked on the door, and when she opened it, he bent down and kissed her. I had never felt such a rage build up in me over a woman. After more long talks and late-night heated discussions, we were able to work through this situation, put it behind us, and move forward in our relationship. I finished my Advanced Course, and we had orders for SHAPE, Belgium. I flew to San Antonio, and things were still a little rocky because of the hurt that we both had. Shalita was working at a restaurant when a Mexican worker sexually assaulted her. He grabbed her, but she was able to fight him off. He fled, and the police were never able to find him. All of these things were going on before I got back, so when I did get back home, I knew my wife and girls were happy to have their husband and father back. We packed our stuff, and the movers came and shipped it to Belgium. During this time, we took a road trip to Augusta to visit Miranda's family before we headed overseas. It was going to be a 3-year tour, and we didn't plan on coming back often, as the plane tickets were expensive for six people. We took our time and enjoyed our road trip to Augusta. Once we got there, we visited her family and said our goodbyes before heading to Atlanta to ship our vehicle.

CHAPTER 29
Belgium

WE LOADED UP all of our luggage, and our family of seven was at the airport, ready to fly to Belgium for our next adventure in life. This would be the first time our entire family would see Europe. We would be here for at least three years. All tours to Europe were three years if you brought your family. These were called "accompanied tours" and were only offered in locations that were not hostile. This was going to be a great opportunity for my wife and girls to see other cultures and countries that most people dream about. We were excited and nervous at the same time. We wouldn't have a vehicle for about 30 days after we arrived, and we didn't know what to expect. This was going to be the ultimate test of our marriage because once we got there, we were told that finding a home would take about 60-90 days. Most people with smaller families were in the hotel for about 30–45 days. In Europe, most families are smaller, and it's harder to find larger homes. We would be in a 2-room hotel and have to eat fast food the entire time. The hotel we were in wasn't anything fancy and looked very run down. We didn't have a car and had to walk or take the train everywhere we wanted to go. We would eventually rent a car, but it didn't fit all of us, so Shalita would have to help and watch the girls when we needed to run errands.

You could sense the hostility in the air of the hotel with couples. Some couples divorce, or their spouses return to the United States. When you put a family together in a small hotel room for a long time, it's like putting animals in a cage with no breathing room. Many men would tell their wives what to expect or how to do things so they would be prepared, but unfortunately, they wouldn't listen. Even during the briefings, we would relay these messages to our spouses when they told us that we would be walking long distances on gravel and stone streets, uphill, not suitable for smaller kids or strollers. Some listened, and some didn't, which caused even more friction among the couples. It was a rough time until you finally got into your home and your vehicles arrived. Until you had your possessions, you felt like you were in prison and limited in what you could do. Being in the military, the soldiers were used to these things as we trained for rough situations, but the spouses and kids, on the other hand, were not used to them at all.

The first time we ordered a pizza, it shocked us as the pizza was not cut at all. In Europe, they don't cut the pizza unless you specifically ask. It's the same thing for fish. They leave the head on unless you ask for it to be removed. It was a culture shock for many families, especially those that had never left the United States.

We finally found our home, which was about 20 minutes from SHAPE. It was an older home with five bedrooms, two living rooms, three bathrooms, a kitchen with small appliances, an attic, and a basement. The floors were checkered, and the walls were maroon brick with pre-hung curtains that didn't match anything. There was also a fireplace in one of the living rooms and an office room. It wasn't anything spectacular, but we were happy we found a place and didn't have to be cooped up in the hotel any longer.

Things were very different in Belgium, including the way you paid bills. We would have to exchange our money for euros and stand in line at the locations to pay our bills if you couldn't set them up online. We learned the hard way about the heat as our home had small furnaces in each room linked to a 5,000-liter mazut tank in the basement. When we drove past homes in the winter, you could see families sitting at the dinner table with full winter coats, scarves, and gloves while eating dinner. We thought that was very strange. We would turn our mazut tank up and heat the entire house, making sure we were comfortable. The first bill came, and it was for about 1600 euros, which was the equivalent of about $1,200.00. We didn't know about mazut oil; the more heat you use, the more mazut oil you use. This was the first and last time we had a bill that high. We put on our winter coats, scarves, and gloves and did as the Belgians did from that day forth.

The unit wasn't bad, and everyone seemed to get along well. The bad part about SHAPE was that it reminded me of Mayberry. Everyone knew each other and they knew everyone's business. People had to go to Chievres Air Base to get groceries or use the PX for items that were needed. Families would sit in the food court and watch as everyone walked past the food court. You could always tell when people were new. This was like their weekend rituals with their families. It was very weird. The good part about SHAPE was that it was centralized in Europe. This meant that all key places were very close, and flights were cheap through Ryanair. Paris was a little over an hour away, the Netherlands an hour, Luxembourg an hour, and Germany 2 hours. This had good and bad sides to it. As we were helping a missionary couple get their church going, it seemed they were always late to the service every week. We would invite people to service, but it was beginning to get very frustrating after a while. The couple would go to Germany and then call us to tell us they were running 45 minutes behind schedule. When the young man would preach, he was very nervous and always took a drink of water. I guess this was his comfort reaction to calm him down. They would continually play the same song over and over, and I was getting tired of it all. My wife and I were making the announcements, and I was running the sound. Miranda and

I discussed it and thought it would be best to leave the situation. We felt they were taking advantage of the people. They were only overseas to travel and have fun. They didn't seem to be about reaching people for the kingdom. Our family took ministry very seriously, and we didn't want to have anything to do with what was going on. Not long after we decided to part ways, we found our new church home in Brussels, Christian Center-Church For All Nations. This church was amazing and definitely a church for all nations. They had people from all over the world that attended the service. One of the highlights was meeting Philip's brother during an event I was doing at the church. Philip was the founder of the biggest Christian website, called Rapzilla. It is really a small world. As we got settled in, I started back writing and promoting my music. I performed at local Belgian clubs and eventually throughout Europe, including Germany, the Netherlands, Portugal, and Spain.

I began meeting other Belgian Christian artists, and they began inviting me to their various events throughout Belgium.

Everything was falling into place again. I was working on my new music and putting together more events, such as Christian Hip Hop tours. My wife was a part of PWOC (Protestant Women of the Chapel) on SHAPE, and she was putting together jazz and poetry events on base. Our girls were going to the American school on SHAPE. Jasmine was attending the Belgian Pre-School, and she started learning French because that was the only language they spoke at the Pre-School. We visited so many other countries with our families and created lifelong memories. Our girls could experience places such as France, Germany, the Netherlands, Spain, Ireland, Luxembourg, Greece, Italy, and Portugal. I was being booked for concerts all across these countries, and my wife was able to travel with me. We had an amazing time and a wonderful adventure visiting these various locations. We learned so much as a family and enjoyed the different cultures. We didn't take any of it for granted.

I put together a few tours and connected with some American churches in Germany. We did some of the biggest Christian Hip Hop events they have ever had. I teamed up with National Recording Artists Canton Jones and JayMay on the first tour in Germany, which was a huge success. I never thought I would become good friends with one of the first artists I heard do Christian Hip Hop, and now we were touring together. I also met a dance crew that went by the name of Shacah Crew. This was one of the best Hip Hop dance crews in Belgium. As we became close friends, we worked more together. We did a music video for one of my songs. The main guy was Emanuel, and his parents pastored a church. He was very talented. He could sing, dance, and play drums. He was also a photographer and videographer. I was blessed that he was able to do a photo shoot for me for my new album and promotional items. He also designed one of my t-shirts. The next tour we did featured FLAME and UK recording artist Dwayne Tryumf. We had an amazing time with these guys and did multiple dates in Belgium and Germany. I built lifelong relationships with many of the pastors and some of the church members stationed in Germany.

Our family took a trip to Edelweiss Lodge and Resort in Germany, where we met Pastor Holland. Some of the great pastors we teamed up with opened their churches to allow us to bring in something that was outside of the box. They took a chance, and the outcome was very beneficial for their congregation and members, especially those that were new to the faith. As they saw Christian rap artists share their gifts, it encouraged some of them to pursue their musical gifts and talents. Many of them are still going forth in their gifts today. It was a beautiful site to see all of this coming together and connecting people from Belgium and Germany.

My wife was growing in the Lord and learning about precept-upon-precept studies through her PWOC group, where she met some key influential women leaders like Beth Moore. I was excited to see her go forth even more in her gifts and callings through the ministry there at SHAPE. She met some beautiful-hearted women with whom she has stayed connected to this day from different countries. The great part about SHAPE was that it was a NATO base, so different militaries were working together. Many of the spouses of the soldiers connected with each other as more of a support group to lean on and get through difficult times such as missing family, etc. We went through a period of missing the United States and decided to visit Disney World. We had already been to Disney World Paris, but we wanted to return to the United States. Someone told me I could do a "hop" through the military flights back to the States, which would only cost us $27 for the entire family. I couldn't pass that opportunity up and signed up, hoping it would work. If I took a traditional flight, I would have to pay about $1,200.00 per person. When you multiply $1,200.00 by 7 people, you get a lot of money. Prayerfully, we were able to get on the flight. It took us going to Belgium to come back to the States to visit Disney World in Florida. This was my girls' first trip on a C-130 aircraft. This was nothing like a commercial plane. They had seats across the sides of the plane, and the middle had a huge open space. Many people laid out blankets and played games with their kids to pass the time, as it was a long flight. This is how families save money on flights back to the States. The only issue is that you were not guaranteed to get a seat on the flights, so you had to plan accordingly. We enjoyed Disney World and had a blast. The girls had a great time, although it was blazing hot in August. Our flights went smoothly, and we didn't get delayed at all. We were able to fly in and back to Belgium without any issues. That was a huge blessing.

During our last year in Belgium, things started to get a little rocky with Shalita. She was a senior and was graduating high school. One of the pastor's wives tried to work with her and help her study for the ASVAB. She would use her personal time to help Shalita for free because Shalita didn't have a plan for college. She wanted to see Shalita succeed, and she had a heart for the teens. My wife and I were frustrated because she would lie around the house, back talk, wouldn't help out or do chores, treat her sisters like crap, and had a very bad attitude. We couldn't have her sisters watching this behavior as they were still young and growing. Once she graduated, we gave her chance after chance to get things going, but with no success. She didn't want to do anything and even failed the ASVAB on purpose. Shalita was very hostile and even tried to physically jump on me. I had to take her down and pin her to the ground until she calmed down. My wife was fed up with her behavior and attitude. One day, while I was at work, I got a phone call from Miranda. She said she was buying two airline tickets to take Shalita back to San Antonio the next day. I was confused because plane tickets were not cheap, but we were blessed to make good money while we were stationed there. She told me she would fly back with her, buy her a laptop, set her up in an apartment, and pay her first couple of months of rent. Miranda had enough, and we had our younger girls coming up behind her that we had to raise. There was nothing else we could do for her at this point. Miranda was frustrated, and this was the last and final option. I was shocked but agreed and supported her decision. I knew this had to be one of the most difficult decisions a mother could ever make. I had never been through anything like this before, so I didn't know how to react or what to say. I supported her and kept quiet so I wouldn't say anything I would regret later.

Times were rough during our last year in Belgium. However, we were able to stick it out and survive by leaning on each other, as families are supposed to do. It was a hard season for Miranda, letting go of her first child and hoping she would come to her senses and make something of her life. She was constantly worried and held a lot of anger towards Shalita and me. All the years leading up to this moment were doomed from the beginning because of how things started with us. I wasn't around Shalita much and didn't know how to be a father to her. I made many mistakes, and I made many great choices, but I never gave up. I had so much bitterness and anger toward Shalita from how she treated her sisters and the way she treated us as her parents. I didn't know what to do and never had anyone in my life that spoke life into me for those particular troubling situations. It took me years to forgive her and let all of the bitterness go, but I was able to do so and eventually move forward in life. I didn't understand that Shalita felt rejected by her biological father, and she always thought that Miranda would eventually get back together with her biological father. She just wanted someone to love her, which we did, but she didn't know how to receive or appreciate the love that people would give her. She would push people away and didn't know how to be thankful for those that would come into her life to help her. She definitely went through her season, and now she was on her own in San Antonio.

I requested to leave Belgium a couple of months early and accepted an assignment to the 1st Special Forces Group in Ft. Lewis, WA. This was a base that you had never really heard of. However, the people that were stationed there loved it. The only complaint that came from everyone was that it rained all the time and it was very depressing. We thought it couldn't be worse than Belgium because we only got two weeks of sunshine during the year. Ft. Lewis was supposed to be very similar to Belgium. We were ready to go and excited to return to the United States. We had fun, traveled often, and made so many great friends in Europe that we are thankful for every one of them, as well as the time we spent overseas.

CHAPTER 30
Back To America

THE TIME FINALLY arrived when we landed back in the United States of America! We flew into Atlanta, picked up our Expedition truck, and drove to Miranda's dad's house. We were in a time crunch to sell the Expedition because we had bought our first custom-made vehicle through the military AAFES Exchange program before we left Belgium. It was a 2011 Ford Explorer. This was the first time both of us had a brand new vehicle. We had come a long way in our credit, and I had moved up in rank in the military, which allowed us to afford it. We had to pick up the Explorer in Atlanta and would be driving it across the country to Washington State. We were so excited to be back home that we went to Wal-Mart in the middle of the night just because we could. In Belgium, everything closes at 5 pm except for the pubs. If you wanted snacks or anything else, you were out of luck until the next day. Wal-Mart was a lifesaver! We were so happy that we couldn't stop smiling for days. When you are overseas, you appreciate the amenities of America so much more. You don't know what you have until you don't have it. We even purchased our first smartphone from the Sprint store and felt lost because we were so behind in time. It was funny, but we were getting back on track in America.

We advertised the Expedition in Atlanta, and prayerfully we were able to sell it within a couple of days. That was all we were waiting for so we could head out. After we visited everyone, it was time to hit the road for our cross-country trip. We took our time and enjoyed every minute of our family trip. We went to Tucson and visited my mom, sister, and brother. They were so excited to see us as we only get to see them every other year. We stayed in Arizona for a couple of days. We had a great time playing laser tag, miniature golf, and many other activities. We wanted the kids to have a memorable experience and have fun. Our last stop would not be so much fun as we tried to find Shalita in San Antonio. Shalita was so far gone, strung out on drugs and involved with a guy that was abusive to her. She went down a horrible path I wouldn't wish on any parent's daughter. We couldn't find her, and as Miranda prayed and asked the Lord for wisdom and clarity, He directed her to exactly where she was located. I didn't know she got up and took the vehicle to go find her as the girls and I were sleeping in the hotel. Our hotel happened to be right behind where Shalita was living. Miranda connected with her and tried to find out what was going on. She wouldn't tell Miranda anything and claimed everything was alright. She wore some dark shades and covered her face with makeup to hide a bruise on her face.

I didn't know what was going on or anything that happened to Shalita. I just knew Miranda was very upset. We set up a time to meet with Shalita and her boyfriend at Dave & Buster's, not far from the hotel. Later that evening, we all went to Dave & Buster's, and as we walked in, we saw Shalita and her boyfriend standing there. I had to be careful about how I reacted because I could ruin my entire career over some foolishness if an incident happened. I was a CW3 mid-level officer in the Army on the way to my new duty station. The last thing I needed was to end up in jail, miss signing in to my unit on time, and destroy my career at my 13-year mark. They don't tolerate incidents with officers and will be quick to kick you out of the military. We wouldn't have any benefits or a retirement check, and we might be discharged dishonorably. As much as I wanted to choke this guy after what Miranda had shared with me, I tried to use wisdom. As we sat at the table and ordered our food, we started to converse. I offered to assist this guy by connecting him with some gang mentors and programs that could help him get back on track. I told him that I would give him my phone number in case he needed some guidance or someone to talk with to keep him on the right track. He was very respectful and seemed to listen to everything I was telling him. He was receptive and interested. I was glad it turned out the right way and was thankful to God for watching over us during this tense situation. Still, something didn't seem quite right, as Shalita appeared hesitant and off track. Miranda mentioned that we would be leaving the next day, and we were willing to give Shalita another chance. She could pack her items and leave with us as we headed to Washington State. Once there, she could get a job and get back on track. She seemed like she wanted to but was afraid to say "yes." We stayed at Dave & Buster's for about 3 hours, and after our discussion, we told Shalita we would wait for her to call us and let us know her decision. We were leaving the next day, so she needed to let us know ASAP what she wanted to do. The next day came, and we never heard from her. Miranda was worried and knew that it wasn't like her. Since we knew where she was staying, we went to her apartment complex and tried to find where her exact apartment was located. I let Miranda out so she could try to find Shalita's exact apartment, and I drove around the side to see if I could find any signs of them. When I pulled back around, Miranda had found the apartment and was talking with Shalita about her coming with us. She told Miranda that she would stay and come later if she didn't find a job. Of course, Miranda wasn't happy about the decision and knew that the guy probably had some influence on Shalita. She was an adult now, and we couldn't make her leave. Once we returned to the hotel, we packed our bags and loaded the Explorer. We got on the highway and headed to Washington State. It was an awkward drive for the rest of the trip as everyone was worried about Shalita and disappointed that she didn't leave with us. Although she tried not to show it, I could tell that Miranda was extremely upset and worried about her daughter. I tried encouraging her and letting her know she didn't need to worry because Shalita would be alright.

We arrived at Ft. Lewis and checked into our hotel. I in-processed on post and signed into my unit at 1st Special Forces Group. I was assigned to the 2nd Battalion and would be their Property Book Officer. Once I got back to the hotel, we immediately started searching for our next home. We found a nice home in Lacey, Washington, that was for rent. The house was in a nice, quiet neighborhood, and the school system in this area was great. Depending on the traffic, I would commute about 20–30 minutes to work. Our household goods arrived, and we got moved in. The home was gorgeous, with four bedrooms, a large kitchen, a large wooden-floored living room with surround sound speakers, a large second living room, and a two-car garage. This was the perfect place and location. There was a beautiful park around the corner in our neighborhood that the kids would play at. Our family loved our new home and our neighborhood. This was the start of new beginnings as we arrived back in the States. My new unit seemed to be great, and I loved my leadership. I didn't know what to expect working with Special Forces, but it wasn't bad. We worked hard but also played hard. We did physical training on our own at a facility they called THOR. The THOR facility had an astro-turf, weight racks along each side of the facility, a wrestling mat, a rope climb, and cardio machines. We had trainers and nutritionists that helped us get into the best possible shape we could achieve. We had to have this training in place because the Special Forces teams were on constant rotational deployments to the Middle East and Asia. I was able to travel to some places in the Philippines, such as Manila. The other locations were more of the locations where the Taliban were known for trying to train people before conducting attacks. I never saw a unit like this, but it was awesome, and I enjoyed it. During our training classes, we would have catered food from Famous Dave's BBQ, and everything was done on "Big Boy" rules. The only negative side to being in this unit was the memorial services we seemed to go to just about every other week. After a while, so many people became numb to the memorial services, and it rarely affected us anymore. That wasn't a good thing, but it was a mechanism for coping with so much death. I was in the 2nd Battalion for about nine months when I got a call from our lead Property Book Officer at Ft. Bragg. CW5 Jimmy Plater was an amazing mentor to many, and I was just learning about him. As I took over the 2nd Battalion, I was able to get their stats to the top of the entire group, which was a great reflection on the 2nd Battalion. Jimmy Plater noticed this and offered me a position as the Group Property Book Officer. I was up for any challenge, but this unit was extremely different, and I was just grasping my job. He needed an answer within 24 hours and told me to discuss it with my wife. Later that evening, I discussed it with her and let her know the benefits and downfalls, and we decided to move forward with the position.

We were part of a church called Champions Center in Tacoma, Washington, pastored by Kevin and Sheila Gerald. Our family loved this church and everything they were doing. The youth group was amazing, and some of the leaders took to our girls and poured into them. Haley and Jonathan Yaden were some of the key lead influencers in our girls' lives and their walk with Christ. We were thankful for them partnering with us and pouring into our daughters. We made some great relationships at Champions Center and are very thankful for the entire team and staff. After I started getting some events going in Washington, I met a youth pastor named Trevor Gentry, who was a part of the Roots Community Church in Lacey, Washington. Russ Newkirk pastored this church. Russ was one of the coolest pastors I have ever come across. He was a great teacher and influencer and strictly preached the word of God in a real and relevant way that people could relate to. He didn't sugarcoat any messages and gave the truth no matter what people thought. Trevor asked if I could do an event for their youth group, and I gladly accepted. I was excited to partner with a ministry that was on fire for Jesus and all about reaching the next generation. We put everything together and did the event; the youth group loved it. We were able to reach some of the kids that wouldn't open up the traditional way. Other kids came to Christ, and we were excited about the next steps in their walk. This was a newer church, and they needed assistance in some areas. I spoke with Russ, Jason, and Trevor about the needs. We were used to coming alongside ministries and helping them get going. These guys had some great things going, and as we prayed about our decision, we decided to join the Roots Community Church closer to our home in Lacey, WA. I loved every message and felt I was growing more each week. My wife had mixed feelings about the church, but our girls didn't enjoy going there. They loved the people but missed the youth group they were a part of at Champions Center, especially Haley and Jonathan. They didn't have the same type of push at the Roots that they had at Champions Center in the Youth Group because this was a newer church, and they were just getting started. I told my girls to hang in there, and we would make it work. The youth group was going to grow, and they would eventually enjoy the church.

I started making another album called "About Face" and was excited to release it in my new home state. I was connecting with more artists and growing stronger in the word of God, which would reflect in my music. Most of the songs I wrote were inspired by sermons I heard during church services. I was serving in our church, doing great at work, conducting marriage ministry home groups with my wife, and everything was lining up nicely. I met a group called Keno Camp at an event in San Antonio, and they invited me to be a part of a tour they were doing in Arizona. I told them this was one place I had never performed and that my mom, sister, and brother were still there. Not to mention, many people I went to school with were always asking when I would perform in Arizona. I was excited to be coming through Tucson and Phoenix for the event. As the tour dates came and we headed to Arizona, I remember pulling up to the venue. My mom and sister were in a car and passed by. I saw them, and one of the Keno Camp members asked if that was my family. I told them "yes" but didn't seem too excited about it. They asked me what was wrong, and I told them the short version of why I felt the way I did. One thing that I didn't realize is that I still had so much bitterness and anger in my heart toward my mom and stepdad. But Bill, the manager of Keno Camp, pulled me aside backstage and told me that he now understood what this tour was about, and it wasn't them. He told me it was about me forgiving my mom and stepdad. He said I could go on stage, rock the crowd, have a great time, and not forgive them. For the most part, everything would probably be fine. Or I could go outside and gather them and tell them that I forgive them and explain my bitterness and anger towards them. I didn't want to hear what he was saying, but I knew he was right. When I looked in the crowd, my stepdad had also shown up at the event. My stepdad and mother weren't together anymore, but they communicated often. I was extremely nervous but knew what I had to do. I went and got my mom, sister, and stepdad and asked if I could speak with them outside. We all went outside the event venue to the side of the building.

I explained to them my feelings towards them over the years because of the situations I grew up in and how I had forgiven them. They understood, and my mom told me she didn't know what to do and raised me the best she could through what was happening. There was no way that anybody could tell me that God was not real. I asked them if they had accepted Jesus into their lives, and my mother told me she had years ago, my sister did years ago, and my stepdad did within the last year. Praise God! I was excited, and we all joined hands and prayed together on the spot. After we were done, I went back inside and took the stage for my set. As I performed, I could see my mom and stepdad's faces. They both had tears of joy and were proud to see that I made it out of my circumstances and situations. For the first time, I felt like my family was actually proud of me, and this was the first time they saw me perform. As we finished the tour and returned to our families, I told my wife about everything, and she was so excited. I was releasing my new album on my own and didn't have the finances to do so before I left. It seemed like once I let go of all that bitterness and hate, God opened up the floodgates for me. I had a supporter email me and tell me they would send me a specific amount for the project I was completing. The amount she told me was the exact amount I needed to finish and release my project! I could not believe it! He had shown up for me time and time again when I was obedient and did what He asked of me. It was simply amazing. Then I met Antoine Hayden, a videographer with some great prices. We shot the intro "About Face" and "Suited Up" videos that we put out, and they did very well. I had custom-made "About Face" shoes, shirts, posters, wristbands, and so much merch for the supporters. I teamed up with brothers I met along the way, such as Johnny B and his wife Angie, Willie Will, Prawphit On

Point, Terrell, and Marquis. Visionary Beats radio was a huge supporter, and everything was going great with the new release. I was able to record the project with DJ Phinisey in Tacoma and even featured Haley from our former church, Champions Center, on a song about sex trafficking. It was time to release About Face!

While working on my music and upcoming tour dates, I was also learning about the new position as the Group Property Book Officer. The guy I was replacing was fired, and I was expected to come in to fix a huge mess. I assessed everything and talked to my team. Bill Holley and Richard Cosner were my contractors and main support guys I leaned on heavily. These guys were extremely hard workers, and I wouldn't trade them for anyone. We were able to put a plan together and distribute over $25.7 million of equipment that was sitting on shelves and supposed to be with the Special Operations teams in the battalions. We told all the battalions that they had 30 days to devise a distribution plan and pick up the equipment. We cleaned the warehouse and turned our shop around within five months. We decided to compete for the United States Army Special Operations Command Supply Excellence Award as a team. As the group was known in the past as the worst logistical unit across Special Operations Command, we were bound to get rid of that stigma. We prepared and worked hard, and as the competition began, we were inspected thoroughly on our record-keeping, warehouse, policies and procedures, cleanliness, and the equipment that was either on hand or on order. All of the groups that were competing were inspected, and the results came back. The 5th group was no longer the reigning champions, but there was a new sheriff in town named the 1st Special Forces Group Property Book Office.

We won the competition, and our group was now known as the best across the United States Special Operations Command. My NCO, SFC Northcutt, Richard Cosner, and Eddie Holley were instrumental in making this happen. We had a plan, and I was able to motivate my team to the best of my abilities, which assisted us in winning this award two years in a row. While we were competing and winning awards at work, I was also competing and winning awards as a Christian Music Artist. I was selected by the Prayze Factor Awards based out of Atlanta as Artist of the Year, Song of the Year, Album of the Year, and

Christian Hip Hop Artist of the Year. I was learning so much in the music industry while competing for awards and attending award shows with some of the biggest names in Christian music, such as Toby Mac, Kirk Franklin, For King and Country, Jamie Grace, etc. I was selected to perform at some of the largest Christian Music Festivals across the country, such as the Hills Alive Music Festival.

I was able to attend the largest Christian Music Award Show called the Dove Awards, as well as the Stellar Awards. My eyes were being opened, and I was exposed to many things I was not expecting. During these times, I was exposed to so much corruption and sin within the Christian Music Industry. I saw the same artists that were on stage glorifying God come off the stage and act like they had nothing to do with Christianity. I witnessed some of the top musicians in the industry holding hands and kissing the same sex in the hotel lobbies we were staying in. Some of the award shows I was a part of would nominate you, but you were guaranteed not to win unless you paid out so much money or signed up to be a part of some Christian Music Club that you would never use. So many things I saw on this journey were discouraging me and made me wonder why I was doing what I was doing. Yes, I was making pure music for the fans and supporters, but I didn't want them to get lured into this corruption and world of sin that was supposedly leading people closer to God. What I was witnessing was that everything was about money with these organizations, award shows, and artists. This was very unfortunate, and I was very frustrated with the industry. I know that there is no sin greater than another, but when I see these artists that are supposed to be proclaiming the name of Jesus in everything they do, turn around and spit in God's face with their actions, it triggers certain feelings within me.

I received a call from Jimmy Plater while I was at work. He asked me if I wanted to take a position in Tampa, and he needed to know ASAP. I thought he was talking about somewhere in Afghanistan or Iraq, as we tend to name the camps after American cities. He laughed and told me that it was Tampa, Florida. I immediately agreed because my wife and I discussed retiring from the military in Texas or Florida. We have never been to Tampa, but that was one location on our list that we wanted to live in once we retired. We loved Florida and the warm weather! Not long after we accepted the position in Tampa, we received our PCS orders and would be leaving within a couple of months. Our entire family was excited and ready for our next chapter in life!

CHAPTER 31
Tampa, Florida

WELCOME TO TAMPA! After several days of driving across the United States, we finally arrived in Tampa, Florida! We were excited to see what this next chapter of life would bring. The first thing I saw as we checked into our hotel was a snake on the mat at the entrance! I don't do well with snakes, and this wasn't a very good start to our new venture. I don't mind alligators, spiders, etc., but snakes are definitely the worst! As we got settled into our hotel, we had to decide whether we were going to rent or buy a home. Our original plan was to rent a home, but our focus started to change once we started looking more into the VA Loan program and seeing how easy it was to buy. This was where we wanted to retire, so why not go ahead and buy our first home? As we decided to buy, we looked at different homes every day and narrowed our search to our top 5. After about two weeks, we selected a home, began the paperwork, and submitted it to our Realtor. That night, as I went to bed, I had a dream that showed me that the home we selected was not the right home for us. It was very strange and detailed, as we had already signed the paperwork. When I woke up, I told Miranda about the dream, and she was also shocked. We decided to go out on our own to a location I looked at when I came TDY to

Tampa for the first time. We saw a brand new community, and they were building new homes by Lennar in a new development. We walked through the home, and it was everything we wanted. It was beautiful! That night, around 9 pm, I called my Realtor and asked if we could see the home we chose one more time. He told us that it was not a problem. We met at the house, and something didn't feel right as we walked through. The house was nice, but something was off. We went upstairs, and as I leaned against the rail, the whole rail moved. We were shocked! Our Realtor told us that was not supposed to happen and it was a structure issue, which meant we could get out of our contract. We were released from our contract on that home and ended up getting our brand new home built by Lennar in an amazing community. We met our friend Pastor Tommy, the head pastor at Crossover Church in Tampa. We were blessed to have him come in and pray over our home with us as we moved in right after our anniversary in August!

I signed into my unit at Special Operations Command Central (SOCCENT) command. As I was in-processing and seeing how things were being run, I realized I was again stepping into a huge mess. They were missing 478 supporting documents and other key documents for two years! I was taking over another huge problem, and it was time to refocus my staff and get things back in order. I noticed that some of the guys were comfortable and complacent about doing things the way they wanted them to be done. This didn't mean it was necessarily done right, which was why some of the documents were missing and things were not being done properly. It was like an old dog stuck in its ways. I pulled everyone in for a meeting and told them the plan and how things would be done. One particular individual murmured and complained to the other workers.

He was like an infectious disease to the team. This led me to fire one of my workers for the first time in my career. Once we got rid of him, the rest of the team knew I meant business, and we didn't have any problems going forth. We set up a system, got things in order, and passed all of our inspections with a commendable rating, which is the highest rating you can get. As the team began to see what I was doing and the reasons behind it, they understood and began supporting me as I implemented key policies and procedures to ensure everything was running smoothly and properly like it should have been. As we got everything in order and on track, we got a new J4 Directorate that came in and wanted to change everything around. He wanted to move my entire shop into the building they were in, which didn't make sense, as we were in a warehouse and would need to track our incoming equipment. We also had a place to lock up sensitive items, which he didn't understand. I tried my best to keep my team motivated and thinking positively, but I could see the morale quickly declining. After a year of getting everything back on track and in order, we now had a new guy coming in and throwing a wrench in all our hard work. Between traveling to countries such as Qatar, Iraq, Jordan, and UAE regularly to ensure our equipment was being tracked and shipped, now I had to deal with this guy who didn't have a clue about our operations but wanted to change it. I had a problem with that, and I didn't take too kindly to someone messing with the people that worked for me. I had contractors from Lockheed Martin overseas in various locations and my team in Tampa. We all had a strong bond, and I was ready to fight for my people. Eventually, we came to a mutual agreement, but our entire team was moved into the same facility as everyone else. This didn't make sense because we would get package shipments in on a daily basis. We dealt with it and continued to do great work. I would consistently fly in and out of the country to various locations in hazardous areas across the world.

There were times I was sitting on an airplane ready for takeoff. The sirens would go off, the ramp would close, and they would black out our plane. We were sitting ducks as rockets and mortars exploded around us. This was one of the reasons my anxiety and claustrophobia got worse. Other times, I remember sitting in our vehicle in backed-up traffic. A lady walked up yelling at our car with what looked like a baby in her arms.

During these times, it was common for people to blow themselves up just to get recognition on the news for killing Americans. There are so many things I have seen throughout my career, including being shot at by gunfire and RPGs as we flew over the middle of Baghdad in a helicopter. After a while, these things became normal to us and weren't as scary. I would keep many things to myself and try not to bother my wife or anyone else about what I've seen and been through in my career. I would keep everything bottled up and deal with it all internally and through making music.

During this timeframe, I began to build a brand called "The Experience Entertainment."

We would still travel around the country doing Christian Hip Hop events with our team. I met a few guys out here that were killing the scene. 2nd Chaynce, Marty-X, Loso, Petey The

Disciple, and a few others. We bonded, and I told them what I did as an artist and promoter. I ended up signing Second Chaynce, Petey, Boy Wonda, and Marty-r X. I also had my close friend C-Micah and King Wes on the roster. My first show was with Canton Jones, where we had roughly 300 people at the event. This was great as a first event so people could see how we do our events with excellence! We continued doing local shows and concerts, releasing more music, conducting interviews, and attending award shows. I was invited to Pastor Myles Munroe's church in the Bahamas for the Prayze Factor Awards. I was up for five categories. I flew my twin daughters out to this event with me, and we had a blast.

I ended up winning five categories and bringing the trophies back to Tampa. This helped our brand and image as a front-runner in the Christian Hip Hop community. The next event we put on was with National Recording Artist "NF." We also had Canon and a few others perform this evening as well. This event had about 600 people from all across Florida! We continued to prosper in the CHH community and Tampa, building this brand. Unfortunately, all good things must eventually come to an end. Or at least a new season. Some of the artists began to fall away and stray from the core of what we built our company's image on. Some went into another music genre and were doing things we would not promote on the Christian side or with our brand. Others went back to raising their families, about which we still talk to this day. Out of all of the artists on the roster, the one that remains true to this day and has not changed one bit is Boy Wonda, aka Junior Mariner. Junior has always been my A1 since day 1. His heart and passion for people and music are still moving forward to this very day. I am excited to see what God does with him in the near future. He has been consistent and faithful in everything he has done.

In 2016, I was pinned as Chief Warrant Officer 4! This is a great achievement as there is only one more rank to achieve in the Army Warrant Officer structure, which was CW5. A few months after pinning CW4, I was told that I would have to PCS within about a year as my position was going away. This was already set in motion before I arrived at the unit. The position was turning into a civilian slot. This same timeframe would be the same time my twins would go into their senior year of high school. I had to think long and hard about my choice, as this would affect my entire family. I did not want them to move during their last year of high school, and we had just bought a house. I also didn't want to leave them again for an entire year with no set destination on where we would be going next. Usually, after an assignment such as Tampa, Human Resources would send you to one of the worst duty locations because they think Tampa is a chill spot. Yes, the city is great. However, during my assignment, I was in and out of the country almost every month. This was far from a relaxed environment. I spoke with my wife and told her I was going to put in my retirement paperwork. I was coming up on 20 years in the military. We loved Tampa. My girls would graduate from the same high school, I would not have to worry about selling our new home, and it was a perfect time. I put in for my waiver to retire early, and to my surprise, about two months later, it came back approved!

The military was a long, fun, rocky, exciting, rewarding, smooth, and adventurous career, but it was time to finally move on. After 20 years and six months in the Army, I retired in April 2017. I was able to obtain my Bachelor's degree from Liberty University right before I retired and was also able to work on my own business idea.

During the timeframe of my retirement, I asked God to show me what I could do to start my own business and make it different from what everyone else was doing. After a few ideas and research, I was able to come up with a Waterless Mobile Detailing Company! This was a brilliant idea, especially here in Tampa, Florida, where it's sunny and people love to keep their cars clean! I vetted the idea and detailed ten cars for free. This led to me getting 60 more customers within a 45-day time frame! My business was taking off, and I was able to start hiring more detailers that I would train. We would take over my entire neighborhood and serve customers around the entire Tampa Bay area. I eventually opened up more locations in Tucson, Arizona, and Santa Fe, New Mexico. This was highly unexpected, but due to the great customer service, consistent 5-star detailing service, and word of mouth, my company expanded and expanded in territory.

This is another reason I know there is a God! Many may say the word "God," but the one I am referring to is Jesus. He took a nobody like me, gave me talents and gifts to reach people across the world and share my story to help those in need. It took a lot for me to remember my story and even more courage to share it. This is definitely not the end of my story, but I pray what you have read up to this point has impacted you in some way and can help you overcome whatever you may be facing. We don't always stay in the storm, and life isn't always a ray of sunshine.

There will be seasons in this life, and we must depend on God to navigate through each season of our life in order to make the biggest impact. I believe in every one of you reading this book. You may not become rich in finances, but we can all become rich in God and His purpose for our lives! If God did it for me, He can definitely do it for you!

About the Author

JASON MITCHELL is a 20-year retired Army Chief Warrant Officer Four. He is an entrepreneur who has started businesses from the ground up, including Mobile Glo, Inc., an innovative waterless detailing company based in Land O' Lakes, FL. He has also owned a coffee shop called Mitchell's Coffee Time in Lutz, FL. He is the CEO and founder of The Experience Entertainment, an events promotion company focusing on concerts, comedy shows, business seminars, and conferences. He is also currently conducting business as a licensed real estate agent. Lastly, he was formerly a Christian Hip Hop artist who has put out over six national albums and won numerous awards, including Artist of the Year, Song of the Year, and Video of the Year. He was nominated to perform at the BET Hip Hop Awards in 2020 through a contest of over 2500+ artists. Unfortunately, COVID put a stop to everything that year, so the event never happened. Jason is a husband to Miranda and father to Destiny, Alexxus, Alicia, Jasmine, and Shalita. His passions in life are seeing his family happy, music, football, being innovative and helping to change the lives of those that are going through similar situations that he has faced and overcame in the past. Jason has touched the lives of thousands of people all over the world, and he intends to continue reaching millions more until his time on earth is up.

CPSIA information can be obtained
at www.ICGtesting.com
Printed in the USA
LVHW070714281222
735949LV00014B/193

9 781662 864926